To JEFF.

Good fortune can be yours.

fu chi fa   12-01-2019

MY GOOD FORTUNE

Memoir of a Chinese Orphan's Success in America

Lu Chi Fa

With

Dr. Lorin Lee Cary

BookLocker

Paperback ISBN: 978-1-64438-609-5
Hardcover ISBN: 978-1-64438-610-1

Published by BookLocker.com, Inc., St. Petersburg, Florida.

Printed on acid-free paper.

BookLocker.com, Inc.
2019

First Edition

Library of Congress Cataloging in Publication Data
Fa, Lu Chi
My Good Fortune: Memoir of a Chinese Orphan's Success in America by Lu Chi Fa
BIOGRAPHY & AUTOBIOGRAPHY/Cultural, Ethnic & Regional/Asian & Asian American | SELF-HELP/Personal Growth/Success | BUSINESS & ECONOMICS/ Entrepreneurship
Library of Congress Control Number: 2019903748

Acknowledgment

I have to thank many people for my good fortune. Big Sister's counsel when I was a child encouraged me to be strong and helped me face the difficulties I confronted later in life. The Morro Bay Chamber of Commerce welcomed me to the community and has encouraged me over the years.

Karen Grencik urged me to tell the story of my childhood, transcribed it, and found the writer, Becky White, who so skillfully shaped that story into a book, ***Double Luck: Memoirs of a Chinese Orphan.*** I am deeply grateful to these two women for adding so much value to my life. Azul Hull generously donated copies of the book to several Chinese libraries.

Customers at The Coffee Pot, members of my Friday Supper Club and the readers of my memoir suggested that I continue the narrative. Margot Silk Forrest served as a research and editorial consultant in the early stages of ***My Good***

Fortune. My good friend Milt Carrigan has handled innumerable tasks over the years. Milt, Craig Dahlberg, Vicki Leon and Joy Cary critiqued the draft at different points. Dr. Lorin Lee Cary interviewed me a number of times, then substantially revised and expanded the manuscript.

Table of Contents

FOREWARD

Morro Bay, California, where I've lived since 1990, is about mid-way between Los Angeles and San Francisco, and a lifetime away from my childhood hell. Orphaned at the age of four, I survived brutality and starvation in China during and after World War II. At one point a relative sold me for two sacks of rice. In 1951 I fled to Hong Kong for a better life and begged on the street to survive. I eventually made my way to Taiwan and in 1969 immigrated to the United States. I told that story in **Double Luck**: **Memoirs of a Chinese Orphan**, which in 2001 won a gold award from Parents' Choice Foundation.

The central message of this second memoir is that despite poverty and hardship we still can succeed. Even if we lack education, we can fulfill our dreams by setting aside negative excuses and working hard. Setbacks will occur in our lives, but how we react to them, through our actions and attitudes, can lead to joy and eventual success.

This book adds details about my life before I immigrated to America. It follows my quest to create good fortune, the culmination of a childhood yearning to escape poverty and hunger and live in a country where no one had to swallow sorrow to survive. In the United States, I believed, I could be a success. And that has happened, in spite of multiple problems and the lingering effects of childhood abuse. Today I'm a respected citizen of the community in which I've owned a restaurant for nearly three decades.

1
BE OPTIMISTIC

I was barely three years old in 1944 when my parents died within a few months of each other. A careless herbalist poisoned my father. Malnutrition took my mother, though perhaps it was really grief. These were crushing events for a little boy. It was a time of war, starvation and homelessness in China. Japanese troops occupied our country even as a civil war raged.

None of my father's kin or even my own four adult brothers and sisters could or would take me in for more than a few days or months at a time. They had families of their own and not enough food, or in some cases compassion, to feed another soul. No arms comforted me when I was sad, lonely or fearful. And I was painfully hungry almost all the time. So were a lot of other people in China in those days, but I believe a child's hunger hurts more.

When I was five my sister-in-law sold me for two sacks of rice to a Communist village leader. My Oldest Brother assumed I would have a good life with this man. His wife just wanted to get rid of me. Looking back, I know they desperately needed the food and the money the rice would bring when they sold some of it. At the time I hoped that at last I had found a family of my own. I could not have been more wrong.

My new "father," a middle-aged man, had just married a woman with a twenty-year-old son and he wanted a younger boy he could train to be obedient to him. Since he now had two sons, he said he was twice lucky. That was how I got the nickname "Double Luck."

Yet I was anything but lucky. For over a year I was my adoptive parents' slave. I slept on the cold kitchen floor and had little to eat. Hunger filled my days and nights, even when they took me with them as they confiscated food from slightly better off folks in the village. I tried my best to do all that they asked of me, but they complained that I was lazy bad boy. They punished me harshly.

Terrified and alone, I comforted myself by recalling that Big Sister had told me I was a good boy and that I needed to be strong. I chanted these words to myself, and when the opportunity finally arose I got word to Big Sister of my horrible conditions. When I was six she found and rescued me.

This did not end my problems. For the next several years, as the civil war raged and the Communists ultimately triumphed, I bounced from family to family, person to person. There was no stability, no calm. It was a terrible time. Being hungry, even starving, was the central fact of my childhood. I drank a "tea" made from dried lima bean shells sprinkled into warm water and often ate scraps wherever I could find them, even rotted food that made me ill.

In 1951, two years after the Communists had ousted Chiang Kai-shek, I fled with Oldest Brother and his family to Hong Kong and then Kowloon city for a better life. We joined thousands of other refugees in crowded camps. Although now free and safe from the Communists, my trials were not over. My brother could not find work and I supported the family by begging.

That's when my dream of going to America began. When an old man in our refugee camp urged me to give him some rice, I hesitated. And then I remembered that once someone who had saved me from starvation said that caring for others served heaven. It turned out that the man had sons in America, a place, he said, where people were well-fed and didn't need to swallow sorrow in order to survive. When his sons sent him a ticket to join them he told me he would never forget my kindness and that someday I too would see America. I cherished the idea of living where food was not a problem.

For the next two years I continued to beg for the family, but the dream of America never left me. In 1953 we, along with thousands of other Chinese, managed to make it from Hong Kong to Taiwan. Although poverty was widespread there, things were better and I attended school for the first time. I was twelve, the tallest boy in second grade. After only a few months I had to quit and go to work.

Although my earnings helped the family, my eldest brother often beat me. It didn't matter why, or if there was a reason. Even then, I think I realized he was angry with himself. Born with one leg shorter than the other, and forced to walk with an odd gait, I believe he hated his life and took that self-hatred out on me. I still bear scars from the bamboo stick he beat me with.

There were so many different jobs. The one that influenced me the most was at a club for American officers in Taipei. As a busboy and then as a waiter there, I tried to learn English. The language seemed difficult because it was so different from the Chinese and Taiwanese dialects I understood.

The Americans had a language problem of a different sort: they had difficulty pronouncing or even remembering our Chinese names. They solved this in an imaginative way: they put name tags with American names in a basket and had each of us chose one. That's how I got the name Gordon, which is what many of my friends call me today.

I had my own language issues. My long hours prevented me from taking much advantage of the English classes offered. Yet I picked up a few words and did my best to be useful.

I also had my first experience with coffee, which all the officers drank. Excited to try it, I filled a glass half full and added lots of cream and a stick of butter. I was so skinny I thought that the combination would beef me up. Weird, I know. In any case, I drank the whole thing. My stomach was not happy. It was a while before I tried coffee again.

Taiwan at the time was still quite poor, and what I saw while working at the officers' club confirmed what the old man at the refugee camp had told me about Americans. Most important, I encountered a level of living that I'd never before experienced. They lived well.

Image 1 Lu Chi Fa, far right, with other busboys and waiters at Taipei officers' club about 1959

Seeing parents with their children as I worked next to the base swimming pool also made me crave a sense of family, something I certainly did not have with Big Brother. In time I moved out on my own, saved money and continued to fantasize about going to America.

7

The dream persisted when I entered the military in 1961, something all boys in Taiwan had to do for two years. After that I worked in Taipei briefly and then as a waiter at a club for American noncommissioned officers on the huge airbase in Taichung. Once I passed an oral "conversation test," I became a bartender (and eventually the chief bartender) there. And I faced a hard truth. Even if I set aside enough money it would be nearly impossible to get the papers required to leave the country. The government restricted immigration; men younger than forty-five could not emigrate. I accepted this with a sigh and focused on making a good living.

There might have been an obstacle to leaving the country, but not to making money. My years of begging had instilled in me the ability to seek for and spot opportunities, and that's what I did now. The salary at the NCO club, equivalent to fifty cents an hour, was pretty good. The tips were not. Still, the GIs liked me. They were young, close to my age, and they were lonely.

I became friendly with the guys who worked at the base as well as with those who came in from Vietnam for rest and recreation and just wanted to have a good time. I didn't speak English that well, but I tended the bar they frequented. I liked people and used the international language of "smile" well. Sometimes, if we rode the same bus, we'd stop at roadside eating places and I'd introduce them to the local specialties. Watching them maneuver chop sticks was always fun.

Occasionally these friends bought me things at the military Post Exchange, which I sold to wealthy people. But this was not the biggest part of my income. I made myself useful to the soldiers at the club. A notice on the bulletin board let folks know that I could line up taxis or rental cars or suggest places to visit. Doing such favors rewarded me well. If I arranged a taxi ride from the base to Taipei, for instance, the cab driver paid me a commission. I began to accumulate a good amount of money at a time when Taiwan was still quite poor.

Image 2 At age 23

And this set the stage for another important development in my life. One of my army friends invited me to his parents' home in Taichung. He had two sisters, one of whom his mom wanted me to marry. But when I met a neighbor's daughter, everything changed. Vivian was seventeen and I was twenty-four. Her Chinese name, Lai Juie Ying, meant "handsome flower." She was a tall, full-figured country girl, uncomplicated and innocent, and very attractive, a handsome flower indeed. I fell in love and wanted to be with her all the time.

As was the custom, I met her parents at her older sister and brother-in-law's house. Vivian and I got together there many times before we had our first date by ourselves. We rode bikes around Taichung; the first American movie we saw was *Goldfinger*, subtitled in Chinese of course. After the movies we'd go to a Szechwan restaurant where the food had lots of spices to warm one up in this cold province. Every now and then we'd go to a Taiwanese place which featured plain food with little oil or a Cantonese restaurant which featured simple food, steamed or stir fried with little oil. Sometimes we'd just have rice porridge with some side dishes such as salted fish or scrambled eggs with soy sauce.

A few times we experimented by stopping at a coffee shop named South America. Coffee was new to Taiwan at the time and all the young people wanted to try it. Having worked with Americans for so long, I knew how to handle the beverage and so did not repeat the embarrassing disaster of my first try with it years before. Little did I know that decades later I'd own a restaurant with the word "coffee" in its name.

It might seem odd that I'm talking about food as I recall us dating. But remember my childhood. Hunger defined it. I was always hungry. I think that's why to this day I remain so conscious of food.

In any case, after outings with Vivian I'd hire a three-wheel pedicab to drive her home. At the time it might have seemed an extravagance to others. To me it was a way of showing my feelings for her, and making a statement of my good fortune. I had come from nothing and had little education, and now look at me. I was proud of my success and to be with her. I'd been unwanted and unloved as a child. Now it was different.

We dated for six months and got along well. Her parents liked me and my healthy income surprised them because I was still so young. They saw I had ambition and would be a good provider for their daughter.

We were married in 1965 at a fancy restaurant as was the practice then. It was an exciting day. Eighty guests attended, including many of the American servicemen I worked with. During the wedding and reception, Vivian changed her dress five times, in keeping with a Chinese custom for brides. Also in line with tradition, we received a lot of red envelopes with money; the closeness of the relation determined the amount given. Most of this went to pay for the banquet.

Many of my American buddies asked if they could kiss the bride. I agreed after talking with Vivian, although I had my doubts about what kind of kiss they had in mind and whether this was okay for my culture. I remember feeling as if I lived in two cultures at once, the Chinese and the American, and that softened my doubts. Vivian thought it only polite to do as they asked, so she let each of them kiss her on the cheek.

At first we rented a tiny place, maybe 450 square feet. But a year later we built a house of our own on a lot I bought in a suburb of Taichung. This was just the first of my moves into real estate. It was a simple house, compared to the properties I'd later buy in the United States. Construction was relatively cheap then, yet I was only twenty-four at the time and that made it unusual.

"You are so young," a neighbor twice my age said. "You must be very lucky. Good fortune shines on you."

I agreed that it did, and I knew that it was hard work rather than luck that made it possible for me to buy a house when that was beyond the reach of most Taiwanese. The house had about a thousand square feet with two bedrooms, one bath, a great room, a nice kitchen and a big yard. Although we had our own well and running water, uncommon for the time, we had to boil it before drinking. We had a refrigerator, but laundry had to be done by hand and hung up outside to dry. The best thing is that we'd paid the full cost of the house and thus had no mortgage. As a result, I felt accomplished and prosperous.

Vivian's widowed mother moved in with us. Lin Lai Hau was a kind and attractive woman, then in her mid-fifties. She helped clean the house, cook and take care of our two children when they were born. In her free time she often went to the nearby Buddhist temple. Each day we put a small plate of food in front of our own picture of the Buddha as a sign of respect. This was the custom in all Chinese homes. Even my cruel adoptive parents had done it.

Looking back I can see that although I don't do this practice now, many Buddhist notions shape my life. And, of course, I realize that the Confucian values and traditions so central to Chinese culture—especially filial piety and humaneness—also influence me.

Lin Lai taught me a lot about cooking. I can still smell the sesame oil she sprinkled on top of dishes. The food she prepared was so good that I began to invite my American friends to the house for simple dinners. My co-workers often came as well. I was pleased and even excited to share our space with everyone. On those nights my mother-in-law made dishes with American tastes in mind: sliced beef cooked with tomatoes, jumbo shrimp, plain steamed rice.

Sometimes the GIs brought liquor. After dinner they'd play their guitars and sing Western songs or ones they'd written about their home towns, their girlfriends or growing up in America. It was a wonderful, fun time.

I loved the easy friendliness these guys had. These evenings gave me a chance to practice English, and also deepened my desire to get to the United States. Although I told Chinese friends that I understood everything said in English, the truth is that I did not. I have to admit that this was my way to show off. In retrospect I can see too that inviting people to eat with us hinted at the path I would follow later. Back then I just wanted to enjoy myself.

As my opportunities at the NCO club mushroomed, I kept an eye out for other investments. I promised myself that never again would I live in poverty, and neither would my family. Once I'd saved enough money, we bought another house. This one we rented out to Americans for $115 a month, a sizeable sum on Taiwan at the time. Now I was a property owner and a landlord and this deepened my sense of well-being.

Meanwhile our family grew. At the end of 1966 our first child was born, a strong, healthy boy. His Chinese name was Jiun Ming. Jiun means "handsome;" Ming means "intelligent" or "bright." Later he adopted the name Jason. Our second son, born a year and a half later, we named Chia Wen. Chia means "gentle;" Wen means "refined." Later he called himself Kevin.

I was thrilled and proud of my sons, not because they were boys instead of girls, but because they were fine and healthy. Above all, I wanted them to have a normal childhood and not have to experience the kind of cruelties I'd faced. I wanted that for all children.

Around this time I encountered a man whose best friend had immigrated to America. I asked how he'd done that. "I've always wanted to go there, because I'm sure I'd find my good fortune in the U.S." He directed me to Mr. Ching and Good Auntie, my mother's younger sister, predicted that he'd set in motion events that would change the direction of my life. And she was right.

What had merely been thoughts or a wish now became an action plan. I believed that going to America would set our family on a path to a much better future. I knew that we were doing well; I just wanted us to do better. Vivian, by then twenty-two, agreed. She knew I was responsible and trustworthy and at this point she encouraged me to act on my desire. Little did we know how hard a long-distance marriage would be, how long we would be apart, or how this decision would affect both our relationship and the family.

Image 3 In his office at the Taichung NCO club about 1967

With a Taiwanese passport in hand, I bought a one-way ticket to the United States. The visa I'd acquired with Mr. Ching's help, I thought, would be good for five years. I was sure it wouldn't take that long to acquire the funds necessary to move Vivian and our two sons from Taiwan to America.

If I had known then how long the separation would be and the strain it would place on our marriage, I might not have left Taiwan. Yet that is what I did.

2
RESPECT YOURSELF

On the way to the airport Good Auntie told me I could choose to forget the difficult times of the past and be happy, or remember them and be sad. I vowed to live by those words.

I was twenty-seven and it was October 29, 1969, the year of the Rooster. I was going to fulfill my biggest, brightest dream and finally go to America. Grandma had told me that dreams could carry you anywhere you wanted to go. "Follow your dreams," she told me, "and go where you heart leads you." I smiled to myself as I boarded the plane, thinking that this was exactly what I was doing.

I was going to a country where people ate three meals a day and if they worked hard they could be a success. That's what I believed, and I knew that if I labored there as hard as I had in Taiwan then I could save enough money for my family to join me. We could all be free and have a higher standard of living.

The plane from Taiwan took off late, and the engines sounded like demons fighting. Nothing in the world could have dampened my spirits that day. In my childhood dreams, at a time when I'd been helpless, alone and hungry, a mighty silver dragon had swooped down and rescued me. I'd imagined then that the powerful dragon would protect me, and that is how I felt now as this big silver airplane carried me high over the clouds.

I smiled as we hurtled toward distant Honolulu. There I'd go through immigration, then on to Los Angeles where Philip, who I'd met in second grade, would meet me. I had a Taiwanese passport and, most precious of all, a business visa good for five years. It declared I was in the importing business. I was not.

Really, I was just a little Chinese boy inside the body of a man desperate for a chance at a new life for my family and me. Freedom, prosperity and security would be ours if I persevered and worked hard. I had plenty of experience doing both, so I was confident that despite going into a new culture I would be able to make it. My success in Taiwan reinforced that belief. I was so excited I had difficulty keeping still.

I sat in economy class, wearing my best clothes. A reserved Taiwanese army officer sat next to me. We exchanged only three or four sentences during the trip, so I had no way to share my exhilaration. Dinner, to my relief, provided a good distraction. The attendants gave us typical American food, and utensils. I knew how to eat Western style, without chopsticks.

As I cut up my meat, I realized that the officer had not touched his food. But he watched me out of the corner of his eye. I slowed my movements so he could see how to use the knife and fork to cut his meat and spear his vegetables. I gave no sign that I observed his discomfort. I wanted him to save face.

The flight from Taipei to Honolulu took a long, long time. I looked it up the other day; we'd flown over five thousand miles. When we were finally over Hawaii, I looked out my scratched window and saw a river bending and twisting as it flowed to the sea. It reminded me of another lesson I'd learned long ago.

My Favorite Uncle once told me that some people are like rivers: they get broader and deeper as they meander toward the sea. "You are like that," he said. "I promise, as you age your many experiences will make you wiser, and one day you will find your home."

He didn't know that home for me would mean the United States. I did.

As the plane descended to Honolulu I realized I was closer than ever before to my goal. Tears streamed down my cheeks. My good fortune lay ahead. I had $300 in my pocket. My name, Chi Fa, meant "new beginnings." And I had high hopes for the future. I didn't know it as the plane landed, but I also had a very bad piece of news coming my way.

As we exited the plane, my knees stiff from sitting so long, I thought I smelled freedom in the air. My spirits soared. We had only twenty five hundred miles to go to Los Angeles. People seemed friendly, especially toward young children. This was not what I'd experienced as a child. The Americans I met also seemed patient with my limited language skills and eager to help.

I joined the other passengers in a long line to have our papers examined. When it was at last my turn, I learned that my visa would allow me to stay in the U.S. for only thirty-eight days, not five years as I had thought. To do that, the customs officials politely told me, I'd have to have a different kind of visa. I was frantic. My heart beat fast and my mouth went dry. By law, in less than six weeks I would have to return to Taiwan.

Confused for a moment, I wondered if I should turn around and go back. I took several deep breaths to calm myself. I had a plane ticket through to Los Angeles. And Big Sister had assured me often that I was lucky. "Chi Fa," she'd told me, "Good fortune will find you." I believed that.

I took more deep breaths and made my decision. I'd continue to Los Angeles, handle whatever came up and find a way to stay. Childhood hardships had trained me to be strong and I'd demonstrated many times that I could overcome obstacles. I would have to have hope in myself. I would become fluent in English, save money and send for my family. Life is a chance, I thought. If I didn't seize it I'd lose it. And good fortune, I was sure, would be mine.

When we landed in Los Angeles, the number of planes at the huge airport amazed me, and I was a bit in awe as I gathered my bags and met Philip. We'd become acquaintances in second grade when he was seven and I was a young teen. I had reconnected with him when friends gave him a going away party at the hotel where I worked as maître de. A tall fellow, calm and mature, he'd come to Los Angeles and invited me to stay with him temporarily. I'd gladly accepted.

Still a bit dazed, we went to his studio apartment at Wilshire Boulevard and Vermont Street, a half block from Bullocks Wilshire, a high-fashion department store. I stayed with Phillip for several months, grateful for his pull-down Murphy bed and the low rent of $32.50 a month. In time he moved to Canada and I lost touch with him. But that was in the future, and I was grateful to have a friendly person to host me during those early confusing months in the U.S.

I'd been around Americans before, but not like this. Now I was in a locale quite different from what I was used to and in a culture where people did things in unfamiliar ways. Los Angeles was far bigger than Taichung and much more spread out. Cars seemed to be the major form of transportation, and everyone drove so fast it frightened me. At first, even crossing streets seemed like a dangerous thing to do. In time I got over that fear, but it took me awhile before I bought my first car and explored the area a bit.

What impressed me most at first, though, were the super markets. Taiwan at that time had nothing comparable, and of course I'd not been able to shop at the Post Exchange store on the U.S. military base. Now I wandered in local markets stunned by the sheer abundance of fresh produce and its affordability. And a seemingly endless bounty of many different products filled shelf after shelf. All of this staggered me.

What surprised me too were the homeless. The old man who had told me about America so many years before had not mentioned anything about poverty, so it shocked me to encounter homeless adults in the streets. I remember thinking, how could that be in such a super powerful country? Although I saw no children panhandlers, seeing these men and women triggered memories of living in Hong Kong refugee camps and begging for change and food.

In Taipei the distance between rich and poor seemed small by comparison with Los Angeles. Huge mansions surrounded by beautiful grounds graced one area of the city, while in another people lived in small houses or rundown apartment buildings. Yet no matter where I went in those early days, most people were friendly and in general the living standard seemed much higher than in Taiwan. This was indeed my good fortune.

After one week, I started looking for work. Thanks to the busboy and bartending jobs I'd had at American military clubs in Taiwan, I spoke and understood English just well enough to get by. For now, I thought, English language lessons would have to wait. In order to succeed, work was the priority. That was the key to success, and I was determined to do that. I just knew that I could.

I went to a private employment agency, worried they'd ask for my work visa. Fortunately, they did not. They didn't even ask about my experience. They simply sent me to be a houseboy for two wealthy men who owned an elegant home in Coldwater Canyon. They must have figured that being Chinese I looked like a houseboy and thus would do.

Things went well at first. My employers were polite, but loneliness was my constant companion. I am a people person and since both men were out during the day, I was alone in the big house for hours. Although they never specified what I was to do in more than general ways, I dusted, vacuumed, cleaned, polished, mopped, made the beds and did the laundry. I missed my family.

Two weeks after I started, the men threw a big Thanksgiving party. I knew about Thanksgiving food and traditions from my jobs at the officers' club as a teenager. I'd thought of the officers then as father figures. They had looked proud and important in their uniforms, and I'd vowed respect one day would me mine too. I'd not give anyone an excuse to look down on me. So when some fifty well-dressed and friendly men arrived for cocktails at my new job, I had warm memories.

Two other employees helped with the party. I served drinks and took care of the buffet table. After two hours the first round of guests left and we served a traditional turkey dinner to twelve close friends. Name tags at each chair indicated who should sit where. One of the two at the head of the table said "Mrs.," which confused me as only men were present.

"There's no Mrs. Here," I said to one of the other helpers.

He smiled. "You'll understand soon enough."

I was twenty six and naïve, but eventually I did understand.

The party didn't end until around one in the morning. After the men went upstairs I washed the dishes, put them away and straightened the kitchen and living room. I went to sleep at three and rose at seven to complete the job. The living and dining room floors were still a mess, so I started vacuuming. I thought seeing everything clean would please my employers. That was a huge mistake.

A few minutes later, the angry husband stormed down the stairs, his face red. Jabbing his hand at me, he shouted at me to stop. "Didn't you hear me page you?" he yelled. "I paged you twice! You woke us up! What's the matter with you? Don't you know any better? Are you stupid?"

Of course I hadn't heard the pager beep because of the vacuum. A flush of shame crept over my face. I recalled my adoptive father yelling at me and Number One Brother calling me stupid when I couldn't learn Chinese characters fast enough before my first day of second grade. The rough language also made me think of all the other people who had told me I was a useless, no good, bad boy. I recalled too the cold faces of some people when I'd begged as a child. My head drooped and I felt smaller and smaller.

Then I remembered that I was a grown man and living in America. Big Sister would assure me that I had gotten myself here. I was free. I had overcome obstacles before. I'd stood up for myself in the past and I'd do it again. I didn't have to put up with such cruel and unfair words. This job clearly was not the "good fortune" I'd hoped would be mine.

I raised my head and straightened my shoulders. "I quit," I said. "I've worked hard for you, and should not be disrespected this way."

The man gritted his teeth and paid me $90 in cash for my two weeks of employment. "Go ahead, leave," he said. "Get out."

I gathered my few things and left the house. It occurred to me that while the money seemed like a lot compared to what I'd earned before, that he'd paid me in cash so there'd be no paper trail. I didn't care. I knew I'd been right to say what I said. I'd lost a job, and they had lost an opportunity.

As I walked the twelve miles home to Phillip's apartment, I thought about Good Aunt's suggestion not to remember bad people. I thought too about Big Sister's advice. "Your hardship is just temporary," she had said, "and it will make you stronger."

I sighed as I trudged along, lugging a suitcase that contained everything I owned here in America. This was not the best start to my new life. But I would not let nasty people hinder my success. I would do well in all that I did, I vowed, and then no one could look down on me. First, however,

I had to get another job. And I had to extend my visa so I could stay legal. Or I would be deported. Time was running out.

3
USE YOUR INGENUITY

The deadline on my thirty-eight day visa kept getting closer. Worry about that haunted me. I was rooming with Phillip again, and as it turned out that was fortunate. Miraculously, he had a cousin who told me how to get a six-month extension through the American Consulate in Los Angeles. Just in time I extended my visa. At least for a while longer I could stay in my beloved new country. My anxiety lifted, but I still needed a job.

Then, another stroke of good fortune, the employment agency found me work. Now I'd be a bartender at Rudy's, an Italian restaurant in the Crenshaw area of Los Angeles. Although I didn't know it at first, this was a poor and dangerous neighborhood. Fortunately, while I worked there I didn't have any risky encounters. But the restaurant didn't get a lot of business, and the waitresses were in their sixties and not all that friendly. The place, in short, wasn't what I'd had in mind as the launching point for success. But I was determined to do whatever it took to make money. At least I had some familiarity with Italian food because the American officers' club in Taiwan had had a regular Italian Night with food I liked, spaghetti and meat balls and lasagna.

I worked thirty hours a week for $1.65 an hour, which I knew was below the minimum wage of $2.25. I really needed to earn more, but chose to see this as a stepping stone to opportunity. To cut costs, I ate at work and saved every cent in order to bring my family to America.

In the meantime, I tried to learn more English. I was the only Asian employee at Rudy's and it was hard to communicate with my co-workers, even those willing to talk with me. My grasp of English remained weak, my workdays lonely and I didn't have enough money to explore much. I knew few people who might have been able to show me around or clue me in to short cuts on how to do things. My world was very limited.

Vivian and I wrote every week. In time I advised her that the future was unknown and I didn't know when I could send her more money. I suggested that she rent out one of our houses, sell the other one and move with the boys into a cheaper place so she would have savings and a monthly income. She agreed. That removed one big worry.

Four months later I took some of what I'd saved and bought an old white Chevrolet for $300. I wasn't informed enough to be concerned about reliability, but I was determined to drive to the airport and pick up Bobby. My best friend in Taiwan, he'd been the front desk manager at the Imperial Hotel in Taipei while I worked in its restaurant. We'd gotten to know one another well, socialized and shared our dreams for the future. In time he introduced me to Mr. Ching, the man who helped me get a visa to come to America in the first place. Now Bobby hoped to find his fortune here too. Like me he'd left his wife and children in Taiwan, sure that in America he'd be able to carve out a better life for his family.

Although I'd gotten a California driver's license, I wasn't very confident on the freeways. Cars drove so fast it scared me. But I wanted to do it for Bobby. He'd put me on the path to a new life and I was determined to pay him back. I'd moved out of Phillip's place and rented my own apartment, a third floor walk-up that cost $110 a month. It wasn't fancy, but at least Bobby would have somewhere to stay.

When Bobby walked out of the airport with his familiar big smile I gave him a huge hug. To my surprise he wriggled away and took off his shoes. My mouth fell open when he pulled a white envelope out of each one. For a terrible moment I thought he might be smuggling drugs. But no, each envelope contained $4,000 in U.S. currency. This was a huge amount, equal to over $50,000 in 2018. Vivian had sold one of our houses. I just hadn't known it had happened, and we hadn't discussed how she'd get the money to me.

In any case, this moved us closer toward bringing the family together in the United States. I put the money into a bank and refused to touch it. Well, I did a bit later. I sorely wanted a credit card. When the bank wouldn't issue me one, I withdrew all the cash, tucked it into an envelope and headed off to work with that stashed in a uniform pocket. But that's another story.

I gave Bobby the bedroom in my new apartment and told him he didn't need to look for a job until he was comfortable doing so. For the next three months I supported him. We ate at simple restaurants when I got off work, and I showed him around while he got used to his new country. It seemed the right thing to do.

Bobby had a year of college and a big vocabulary and we enjoyed our time together. That changed when he asked to borrow money so he could bring his family over from Taiwan. I refused as I was in the same boat. Our relationship cooled after that.

But long before that falling out I took him to a private employment agency. The application forms asked us to check "White," "Negro" or "Other." This perplexed us. We were the only Asians applying and we didn't give a thought to race. Our sole concern was getting him a job. Poor Bobby's hands shook while he filled out paperwork. I told him not to be nervous, not to worry, that this was a free country.

As luck would have it, or what Big Sister and Kind Auntie would both call "Chi Fa's good fortune," someone phoned just then to say they needed a non-union bartender. I raised my hand when the agent asked if either of us could tend bar.

"I have a young Oriental man here," he told the caller. "He's clean cut and has bartended before." He nodded as the caller said something and then said "I'll send him right over."

When I heard about the job at Host International, I got quite excited. This would be a real step up from Rudy's. And if it worked out, I figured, Bobby could take my position at Rudy's. And that's what happened.

The agent drew me a map on how to get to the hotel, but I somehow took the wrong bus and arrived late that afternoon for my interview, a restaurant which catered to waiting passengers at Los Angeles Airport. I filled out the application form as best I could.

After he looked over my information, the personnel officer stared at me. That worried me. What did it mean? He eventually stood up and shook my hand for what seemed like a long time.

"Your experience looks good. Congratulations and welcome on board," he said with a smile. "Oh, I see you forgot to put in your green card number. Well, just bring it in tomorrow. You can start then."

Of course, I had no green card. I swallowed hard and told him a white lie. "I'll bring in the green card later. Forgot it today."

He gave me the job anyway; I think he felt a connection with me because it turned out that he'd been stationed in Taipei for thirteen months. Clearly, I had met someone I needed to meet—which is what has often happened to me. Finally I was making $4 an hour! And I got a free lunch each day, American "Chinese" food like fried clams, shrimp and beef. It lacked the spice I liked, but it cost me nothing.

Several times over the next months the personnel officer asked me to bring in my green card. I stalled each time and said I'd bring it in later. I don't know whether or not he believed me, but the situation for immigrants back then was much more humane than it is now. I hoped that I could prove my worth to him and have a better chance of staying.

Work filled my days. To get to Host International I had to take two buses. I worked forty hours a week and the schedule often changed. That meant I couldn't attend classes to improve my English, so I did my best to learn on the job. Customers came into the bar from many countries and other states. They didn't know how poor my English was and they'd talk and talk. I'd smile and nod and ask questions if that seemed the right thing to do. It's one of the ways I've always learned. People appeared pleased that I tried to converse, and some said they hoped to keep in touch. I understood that they were just being polite.

Most of the people I met were kind and friendly. I cringed inside when a few of them talked baby talk, or spoke loudly, seeming to assume that this was the only way to make me understand what they wanted. I swallowed my pride and reminded myself that I was a smart and capable man.

To improve my English I tried to do more than have brief chats at the bar. I listened to the radio and read newspapers, and when possible talked as best I could with my fellow workers. They seemed to treat me as someone special, perhaps because there were so few other Asian employees. On the long bus rides home I occasionally managed to have conversations too. Some people were happy to talk. I gradually got more confident with the language.

But the fact that I did not yet have a green card left me worried and anxious. One of the most awkward moments about this had to do with an immigration officer who came into the bar for a ginger ale before work. In general the attitude toward immigrants back then was much friendly than it is now. And this man, in full uniform, was a good example of that more welcoming point of view. He smiled and seemed interested in starting a conversation.

"So, how are you today?" he asked as I put down his soft drink.

"Fine. All good," I said, and backed a good five feet away from the counter. Inside I trembled. I appreciated his friendliness yet feared my English wasn't good enough to handle much of a discussion and that if he pushed for a talk he'd get suspicious and think I might be illegal. I wasn't, but my six-month business visa had nearly expired and I didn't want the INS tracking me. So I did what often worked in such situations. I smiled and said nothing more. It worked, and he left after a while. I saw him another time in the employee cafeteria and we smiled at one another, and that was that. But it was a constant worry.

During my early months in the United States the freedom with which Americans moved around and the choices they had impressed me, compared to the limited options in China and Taiwan. But if I didn't do something soon, that freedom wouldn't be mine much longer.

After getting suggestions from some other Chinese, I learned that a student visa would let me extend my stay legally. So in 1970 I enrolled in a private business college. It required proof of a high school education, which of course I did not have. I presented my Taiwanese passport and, not wanting to lie, said nothing else.

When I returned three days later, I found that the school had accepted me and that my passport now had a student visa in it. This thrilled me. The college didn't seem to care if students attended classes or completed courses. Its goal, I soon realized, was to enroll students and collect fees. I took English and typing classes. Although I didn't understand most of the lessons, they helped some. I got the general idea and went through the motions to be counted present. I'd been so worried about visa expirations, and now I had more time.

4
TAKE RISKS

For the next piece of good fortune, what turned out to be a key turning point in my life, I must thank my "lucky stars." In this case I mean the Water Horse, the astrological sign I was born under in 1942. Water Horse individuals are said to be highly adaptable, flexible and quite social—and can also be indecisive. That fit my situation. I was getting desperate, unsure what to do. Worry and loneliness were my constant companions. I'd been able to extend my original visa, and then add more time with the student visa. But that would run out in time and my chances seemed slim in Los Angeles of securing a green card, a permanent United States residence and employment permit.

And then, about a month after I enrolled in the business college, Paul Shi called from Denver. We'd become friends in Taichung when he worked at an Italian restaurant. Before I left

Taiwan I'd let him know how to contact me. He'd come to the U.S. months later and now worked at Tommy Wong's Island in what he called the Mile High City.

"How much are you making?" he asked me, which is how Chinese often start talking.

"Union wage," I said, "$4 an hour."

"Well," he said, "there's a job open at Tommy Wong's here and it might be the path to getting a green card."

"Give me the details and I'll be there," I said, my heart racing.

I had taken chances before—standing up to Big Brother and my first employer in the U.S., and for that matter coming to America. Now there was the opportunity to secure the coveted green card, and stop worrying about my status. That's why I did not hesitate to act on Paul's news.

Fortunately, I had three days off work and could check out the opportunity in person. I bought a round trip ticket to Denver. As the plane landed, I saw snow close up for the first time. I was giddy with excitement. In Taiwan snow was only on the highest mountains, something seen from a distance. Here it was everywhere. Although I was now in my late twenties, I felt excited like a child. This, I thought, was something new, perhaps a good omen.

Paul picked me up at the airport and took me directly to the restaurant, a big place with many different themed rooms. Tommy's general manager interviewed me and then Tommy, a short, energetic man, did too. When they offered me the bartender job I said I'd need the $4 union wage, and they agreed. They also said I could order directly from the kitchen, free food from the menu while I worked. Most of the employees ate together. Because the bar was so busy I could not do that. Good fortune indeed! Thrilled and excited, I headed back to Los Angeles.

I gave my two weeks' notice, packed up my apartment and then headed to Denver. I found a place near the restaurant that I could share with a co-worker. The complex even had a swimming pool. Surely this was a sign of good things. It was.

Tommy Wong's was a nice place to work. We wore black pants and Hawaiian shirts, and there was a chance to make good contacts because all kinds of people came in. Most were very friendly. I learned how to make various Hawaiian and other combination drinks, and used the techniques I had acquired in my different bartending jobs. I smiled and listened. And I agreed or disagreed with what people said, depending on what seemed right. If I didn't understand a word or phrase I'd ask the person to explain it, privately.

It was a great year. Given the weather I spent a lot of time indoors. But I mastered driving in the snow and even how to put chains on my tires. In my spare time I visited Boulder, Colorado Springs and even the Coors plant in Golden. Most of the time I hung out with other employees. It was like being part of a big family, and I loved that. I missed my own family to be sure, but this was good. In retrospect, I also see that I still had a problem with English. Being with my co-workers so much didn't advance my understanding of the language.

At times I socialized with Tommy Wong and his assistants. Tommy was a gambler and often traveled to Las Vegas. A high roller, he had come a long way. His story wasn't all that different from mine. He was born into desperate poverty in a small Chinese fishing village brutally occupied by the Japanese for eight years. After World War II ended Tommy left home and worked on a British cargo ship. He shoveled coal, washed laundry and helped the cooks in the kitchen. He eventually landed a "high-paying" $18-a-month job on an old Panamanian freighter. It nearly sank during a major hurricane and when it limped into New York for repairs Tommy jumped ship.

This was in 1951. Like many Chinese who came after him, Tommy worked at a series of low-paying jobs and hid out from the Immigration and Naturalization Service. His various jobs took him from Washington, D.C., to Chicago, Miami, Phoenix and Denver. Once he could afford it, and was legal, he opened a restaurant in Phoenix, then ones in Colorado Springs and Denver. All were Far Eastern themed and had the same name, Tommy Wong's Island.

Besides being an excellent restaurateur, Tommy understood the profound desire of his countrymen to immigrate to America and he was determined to help them. His top assistant Paul had jumped ship with him and been deported years earlier. Tommy brought him back to Denver and helped him become legal. He wasn't the only person Tommy aided. While I worked there he submitted green card applications for eleven of us.

Tommy had a close friend in the Immigration and Naturalization Service who helped him do this. He listed me as a specialty cook since I'd had that experience in Taiwan. Bartending, he explained, was not a job eligible for a green card. Six months later Federal agents interviewed me, and none of the others. The INS rejected them, I learned later, because they had no legal status in the United States. All of them had jumped ship when they had arrived from Taiwan. But I had my student visa. Once again my good fortune persisted. Those classes in Los Angeles saved me. Three months after my interview I received my green card and I was overjoyed.

Image 4 Lu Chi Fa in 1971

But now my happy environment at Tommy Wong's became intolerable. I had worked with one of the cooks at the American air base in Taipei and he had been friendly at first.

39

When he didn't get a green card, he turned on me. The other angry and jealous cooks took their frustration out on me too, saying I was Tommy's favorite, his "golden boy," and spreading other nasty rumors.

At the time I couldn't understand why this was happening, but I knew I wasn't going to accept treatment like that. I thanked Tommy for all his help. I shook his hand and walked out of "the Island" for the last time. Tommy's willingness to assist freed me from constant worry about visa expiration and deportation. He'd given me a new life in the U.S. I promised myself I would not forget and that when possible I would help others too.

Leaving was the right thing to do. Tommy had increased my confidence that I too could realize my American dream. Even though it was my choice, I was sorry to leave the "home" I'd found in Denver. Doing so reminded me of when I was three, kicked back and forth like a soccer ball, going from home to home unwelcome anywhere.

5
DISAPPOINTMENT

Now that I had a green card, I could leave the country and reenter without a problem. Finally, I could return to Taiwan and bring the family back with me to my new country. I had been away more than two years by this time, and I was eager to see Vivian and the boys. We had been writing regularly and I wanted to have them with me. I remembered the early days of our marriage as I prepared to reunite with my wife.

I was nervous, especially about seeing the boys. I had never had any fathering myself so I was uncertain and anxious about how to act with them. The Chinese are not openly affectionate as a rule, so I knew I shouldn't run up and give them a big hug. Still, as my plane landed in Taiwan that's what my heart wanted to do! I didn't feel rejected by the kids; this was a one-sided struggle, within me.

But the trip did not go as I'd expected. The connection between Vivian and me seemed off. We'd been apart too long, or something, I wasn't sure what. I also found myself awkward with the boys, by then three and five. I kept my emotions in check and low key, and they remained that way during the coming weeks.

Vivian was still renting out the house that we owned to American GIs for $86 a month. As I'd suggested, to save money she and the boys lived with her widowed mother in an inexpensive rental in a lower middle-class neighborhood near her sister in Taichung. It had two stories and was quite plain inside. There was one large space for the kitchen, dining room and living room. The boys shared a bedroom.

Most nights Vivian and her mother cooked simple meals for the five of us. After dinner we'd often walk to a nearby park that had lots of open space and playground equipment for the kids. I'd watch them play, but didn't really know how to join in. When we got home we'd watch entertainment on TV, maybe a flute concert or some traditional dancing.

One night my Number One Brother and sister-in-law invited us for dinner. In the past there had been big problems between my brother and me—the beatings, how he'd made me beg for rice or money to feed the family for four long years, and how when I got a real job at age fourteen he'd taken all my pay. That had gone on for three years and I never saw a cent of the money.

When I vaguely referred to these issues, my brother stayed silent, his face flat and expressionless. Guilt or pride, maybe shame, I thought, kept his face frozen. Now that I was independent and free of his control, I no longer felt angry. If anything, I was sorry for him. Because he had one leg shorter than the other, he had always had an unbalanced walk. It seemed to me that his life was unbalanced as well. It lacked joy. I realized then that I'd internalized the Buddhist attitude I'd learned growing up in Taiwan: "Remembering a wrong is like carrying a burden on the mind." I was a bigger man now, not a bitter one. My soul had grown.

As it turned out, it was a pleasure to visit my brother's family. Although my sister-in-law had sold me, she had also taken me with them when they escaped from China, so I had no negative feelings toward her either. I especially enjoyed eating her dinner specialty, lion's head. She seasoned one and a half pounds of ground pork with fresh ginger, cornstarch and egg, shaped a lion's head and deep fried it until browned, then cooked it with Napa cabbage in pork stock for an hour on low heat to tenderize the meat. I had never had such food in my brother's house before and I left feeling grateful.

The days with the family went well, I thought. But I knew little about my sons. Vivian had written me about them often, yet being with them was different. I didn't know what to expect. For instance, one day I bought a chocolate birthday cake for my younger son, Kevin. The cake disappointed me. It was chocolate on the outside but only a white sponge cake inside. My son, however, was happy that I bought it. I had completely misunderstood that our relationship was far more important than an imperfect cake. And although we did family things like sharing picnics in a public park, I continued to feel somehow disconnected from the three of them. Soon I learned why.

Despite appearances and the fact that she'd gotten green cards for herself and the boys, Vivian eventually gave me crushing news. She was not going to come to America with me. "That is your cup of tea, not mine," she said. "I am a Buddhist and I want to stay in my own Buddhist country."

Surprised, I heard her out in silence, and then walked outside to be by myself for a while. I felt hollow. I knew that my years away had damaged our relationship, but I had not expected this. I went back into the house and begged her to come with me. She said no again. I stayed an extra week to persuade her, but she was adamant.

"Taiwan is my culture, my home," she repeated, "and I am going to raise our children here."

Now I understood why we seemed disconnected. Vivian had already made up her mind not to immigrate. She just hadn't told me right away. I returned to the U.S., discouraged and lonely, but with the thought that I'd be back and that they would come with me.

6
BE A PEOPLE PERSON

Back in Los Angeles I rented a one-bedroom apartment for $135 a month on Sepulveda near Jefferson, just a bit north of Los Angeles International Airport. I moved in by myself. I would have preferred to have a roomie, someone I could share the events of the day and life feelings with. But that didn't happen. I chose this location because I hoped to get back my old job at Host International. I thought they'd be glad to see me. These were unrealistic hopes. The man who'd originally hired me was gone. There was no job for me.

But I am nothing if not persistent. I began work as a part-time bartender at the International Hotel near the entrance to the airport. I drove there in my used dark blue Mercury Montego, the second car I'd ever owned. The interior was in excellent condition and, to me, she was beautiful. Thanks to my time in Denver, my driving skills had improved and I had more confidence.

Image 5 About 1975

After a few months, I secured full-time work at the International. It was a huge hotel, twelve stories high with a rotating bar on top. People sipped their drinks and watched the airport runways as planes rolled by. My limited English continued to pose a handicap and no other Chinese worked there. As I recall, by this time I understood more English than I could speak fluently. Still, a few times rude folks loudly embarrassed me in public for not comprehending what they'd said. As I'd begun to do in Denver, I made sure that if I didn't understand a phrase or word I'd ask the person, quietly, to explain it. That helped and I met some interesting people who said they hoped I'd stay in touch with them. It reminded me of my days in Taiwan when the American officers had been so friendly.

Later in 1971 I met Jeff Chow, a waiter I had known at Tommy Wong's Island in Denver. A heavy smoker, Jeff had yellowed teeth and I could smell the cigarette smoke whenever we talked. On one occasion he told me that his new workplace, Eddie's Little Shanghai in West Hollywood on Sunset Boulevard, the only Chinese restaurant in the area, was hiring. I went over and landed a job as a bartender, thrilled that now I would have more people I could talk with.

Eddie Wah was a short, energetic man who wore big heel lifts to seem taller. I really enjoyed working at his restaurant. A lively place, many colorful people hung out there late at night, including reporters, politicians and movie stars such as Dick Van Dyke, Orson Wells and, according to Eddie, one of Charlie's Angels. A lot of marijuana smoking went on in the bathrooms.

I got to know an actor who had been in some movies and lots of television shows, although at first I didn't know who he was and I just can't recall his name. While he waited for his take-out order he'd sit at the bar and talk.

I saw everyone who came in because the bar was at the front and the eating area was in an adjacent room. Once the Chinese producer of the movie *Flower Drum Song* told me that I was handsome enough to be in movies. I knew it was just bar talk. The food served was a pale American version of Chinese. It had little spice. But the tips were good and I continued to add to my savings. I was thankful for the job and ended up staying for three years.

7
IF YOU FALL DOWN, GET UP

By 1974 I'd earned three weeks of vacation and saved enough money to bring my family to the U.S. I planned another trip to Taiwan to fetch them, determined that this time I would succeed. Despite the outcome of my last visit, Vivian and I had been writing regularly and I knew that Jason and Kevin, my seven and five year-old sons, were doing well. Vivian was a good mother and I was thrilled with the prospect of our family being together after all this time. I believed that now Vivian would agree to come with me to the U.S.

But I was wrong. She had not changed her mind. That's the long and short of it. I returned to the U.S. aching with disappointment. The loss felt huge. All those years of hard work and saving, all that loneliness in order to achieve a goal seemed wasted. I tried to not to let the pain feed my soul. But the sorrow stuck in my throat. It was too fresh and too familiar.

Once again I had lost my family. Not from poison and malnutrition, as with my parents, but from years apart, a separation of over seven thousand miles, and perhaps a clash of cultures.

A few weeks later an envelope from Vivian arrived. I opened it eagerly, hoping for good news. But it contained only her green card. I looked at her name filled in neatly and understood that this was her final word on the matter. "See," she was saying, "I will *never* use this." I understood fully then that while our sons would be our sons, we would never be a family in the traditional sense. Never.

This was one of the lowest periods of my life. I tried to practice what Buddha advised: "Do not dwell in the past, do not dream of the future, concentrate the mind on the present moment." It wasn't easy. I went back to work at Eddie's Little Shanghai, from eleven in the morning until nine at night. By the time I got home it was about ten-thirty and I was exhausted. I had a roommate and might have been able to share my pain with him, but our schedules were so different I rarely saw him. I could talk with some fellow workers, but the conversations seemed shallow. So the pain stayed inside me.

As in the past when I'd confronted obstacles I remembered what Big Sister had advised me decades ago: be strong and know that difficult times will pass. You've come this far, I told myself, you will find your good fortune. Determined that I would not let disappointment and hurt stop me, I willed myself to concentrate on the present. Still, I was profoundly lonely and sad.

Although I no longer had a real reason to work so hard, it now became my whole life. I'm sure I was trying to bury disappointment and sorrow and put it behind me. Looking back, I think it was during this time that my notion of success gradually began to change. I suspect I wanted to prove to myself that I was still a good person and could succeed in America, even though I had failed to reunite with my family.

I realized too that I needed to feel secure. What I had previously worked for no longer existed, and that left me feeling unsettled. I started to think about buying my own house. This would be a clear sign of success, and it would be a way to provide more stability in my life. Now there was a reason, once again, to save. I would shape my security; I would not wait for it to happen.

8
WORK HARD AND SWEAR ALLEGIANCE

By 1977 I had built up my savings and a new friend in Orange County persuaded me that it was time to create the security I so desired. Al Martin, a friendly realtor who became a lasting business contact, helped me qualify for a loan to buy a house and later encouraged me to start my own business. He was the first of many realtors who would guide my decision-making about residential and business properties. I felt I could trust him.

Al had a trustworthy face and I believe you can tell a lot from people's faces. The physical abuse heaped on me as a child made me acutely sensitive to other people's emotions and the signals their body language and expressions sent. As a result, I learned early on to "read" the people around me. My experience begging on the streets of Hong Kong and Taipei sharpened this ability, and it's something that has stayed with me always.

In any case, it was a good thing that I met Al because real estate in the U.S. was all new to me. In Taiwan I'd always dealt directly with builders. I hadn't even known there was such a thing as a realtor. When I had difficulty qualifying for a loan, Al looked over my application and nodded.

"Ah, I see what the problem is. You're not including your tips," he said. "Just estimate what you get each year and add that to your income. That should do it."

It did. My loan sailed through and I bought a nice condo in Santa Ana, not far from South Coast Plaza, one of the top shopping malls in the country. I used money from the sale of the house in Taiwan for the down payment. The purchase price of $63,000 was a lot of money, but it was also an investment. I had inherited the Chinese belief that you can never go wrong with property. "Money in the bank," the saying goes, "does little. But real estate has a many fold return."

For me, this was a huge step—my first American home. Surely, I believed, this was evidence of my good fortune, a sign that I could create the stability that had been so missing in my childhood and succeed even if my family plans had not worked out.

The big numbers involved in the purchase made me remember my days as a little beggar boy in Hong Kong. Then I'd brought home the equivalent of fifty to seventy-five cents a day to pay for food and the rent on a one-room shack where I lived with my Big Brother and his family. By contrast, my new condo had three bedrooms, two baths, a large yard and a two-car garage. It was beautiful and very private. I really didn't need that much room for myself. But I knew it would pay off if I sold it. And it was mine, and so different from every place I'd lived as a child.

Because the Orange County condo was so far from my workplace in West Hollywood, I tried to find a job that was closer. The headwaiter at a local Chinese restaurant told me that Quian's in Tustin was looking for a full-time bartender. After a quick discussion of my experience, the Chinese owners hired me on the spot. Rosie and Walter had been in the country for a long time, worked hard, saved money and then opened their restaurant. They spoke English well, as did their kids. I respected them, and was a bit envious as well. They'd succeeded in circumstances similar to mine. Now in my mid-thirties, I knew I could do the same. Their path became a beacon and their restaurant a model for how I too would continue to build my own good fortune.

Although I remained unhappy with my English, my bartending training was good and my language skills strong enough to do the job quite well. I knew how to mix lots of drinks, and I knew how to smile. Because I like people, customers talked to me freely about their troubles. And I could make them feel better. I'd listen, ask questions and nod, even if I did not understand every last word.

The most difficult part of the job was when I had to "86" someone, tell them they'd had enough and I couldn't give them yet another drink. It took me a while to get up the courage to do this, but in time I learned how to do it. "How about a coffee?"

I'd say, or "How about a tea?" Anything to dilute the alcohol. "No," they'd say, "I want a drink."

Image 6 Orange County, about 1978

When I knew the people I was talking to it generally went well. On a few occasions some hot shot resisted verbally with a curse or two. Sometimes other customers stepped in to back me up. I had to be a kind of psychologist doing this and I learned time and again that drunks aren't rational. They're like children, and sometimes like babies.

My experience with heavy drinkers, I see now, served as another turning point in my life. It was one of the reasons I began to think that I did not want to be a bartender forever. Bartending had been good to me, but there were limits to what I could achieve—particularly if I worked for someone else.

I knew I lacked much education, but I had a strong drive and had already achieved much and created a life far different than my childhood. But if I wanted to advance myself and do even better, I needed to do something else. I would have to become my own boss. Buddha once said that "If you do not change direction, you may end up where you are heading." That made more and more sense to me.

Now it was a question of seeking for and finding an opportunity to change direction. Some people have possibilities in front of them, yet never see them. I vowed that I would keep my eyes wide open for chances. Since all my experience was in the food industry, that's where I looked. I was comfortable here and had the skills and passion to drive forward. I wasn't exactly sure what I had in mind, but I talked with a lot of other Chinese about my idea of doing something different than bartending.

As good fortune had it, one of the people I talked with was John Chen, also a bartender and a recent immigrant. Although he worked at a famous gourmet Chinese restaurant in Los Angeles, like me he hungered for a different, more successful life. John was younger and because of my experience he respected me. I liked him too and our mutual quest to succeed and willingness to take risks led us into a business partnership.

We found a vacant restaurant in a little shopping center near Chapman College in Orange County. A lot of retirees lived in the area, so we were excited. Students and older folks, we assumed, would flock to our place. We signed a lease with the owners of the shopping center, improved the kitchen and got permits and licenses to operate the restaurant and serve wine and beer. We hired a chef and put together a simple menu.

In 1978 we opened China Diner, prepared for prosperity. In China restaurant owners are people of status and that's the way we felt. The work schedule, though, was punishing. Seven days a week, from eleven in the morning until to eight at night, John and I waited tables and did everything but cook. We were young, full of energy and optimism. And we were profoundly unprepared.

Apparently I hadn't learned enough working at Quian's. We hadn't researched the restaurant thoroughly. In fact, we really didn't know what we were doing. For the first eight months we had hardly any business. We didn't know how to promote ourselves. Our menu proved too limited. The location was poor. People knew we were green and pressed their opinions and criticisms on us. Vendors took advantage of us. We had to swallow our pride a lot. It did not taste good!

Although things improved a bit over time, the shopping center was too small to generate much foot traffic. After two years of sweat and effort, and an eighty-mile daily commute for John, we admitted failure. It was a painful thing to do. Unlike a bad marriage, where you can get a divorce easily, if you run a restaurant that's not an option. There was no easy out. We could not even sell the restaurant; the earnings had been so poor the place attracted no buyers. So we walked away from the business. Despite our high hopes at the outset, China Diner wasn't worth anything, not even the kitchen appliances. Our failure left John bitter and unhappy with me.

I was discouraged. All I'd wanted to do was make a better living, and instead it seemed that I'd wasted my time, energy and money. This was not what the path to good fortune was supposed to look like. But I refused to wallow in sadness. I recalled what Big Sister had told me as a child that my hard times were only temporary and that they would make me stronger. And they had. I reminded myself of that as I thought about what had happened and learned from the experience. China Diner, I began to see, had been a huge gamble. Our thinking had been immature and the financing weak. Our enthusiasm and big ideas wouldn't have guaranteed success, no matter how many hours we had put in.

In Taiwan at that time such a failure would have limited future opportunities. The belief was that if a man has not succeeded by the age of forty, there was no second chance. But this, I reassured myself, was America. As I gradually recovered my inborn optimism, I told myself I was young enough and had enough energy to try other business ventures. There were plenty of possibilities. And I had always known that being open to opportunity was crucial.

The failure had taught me what not to do, so I'd take my time and avoid the errors that had doomed China Diner. I vowed to prepare more carefully and set aside enough savings to cover living and business expenses for up to eight months. If I did these things, I believed, I'd get back on track and create my good fortune.

For the next two years I worked as a bartender at a luxurious hotel in Costa Mesa. Although I wasn't all that happy with the job, it allowed me to build up my savings once again.

Meanwhile, my desire to have my own restaurant grew and I began to keep my eyes open for another opportunity. Having been terribly poor as a child, I yearned to achieve financial success. That had not yet happened. Worry crept in that I might not make it.

That helps to explain why I decided it was time to become an American citizen. I needed freedom from worry and I needed evidence for myself that I was successful. Even though my family had not joined me, even though my first business venture had failed, it seemed to me that this would confirm that at least I had achieved a big part of my American dream. I could not keep heading in the direction I'd been going.

U.S. law stipulated that I could file for citizenship five years after I'd gotten my green card, which had been late in 1971. I'd filled out the form and submitted it when I was eligible to do so, and had assumed that I'd get a response. That hadn't happened. Months and then years passed, and because I had acquaintances whose forms had been approved in one year or less I could not figure out why my situation was so different. The information on the application was straightforward and not difficult to read. After a while I kind of forgot about the issue until a friend questioned me.

"Whatever happened to your citizenship application," he asked.

"Nothing. I never heard back from the government."

"So what did your lawyer say?"

"I didn't have one. Didn't know I needed one."

"Well, Chi Fa, there's your answer. Get a lawyer to file, and it will go quickly."

I decided not to waste another five years. So in 1983, at the age of thirty-eight, I hired a lawyer and reapplied for citizenship. I'd been in the United States almost fourteen years, yet was still not fully literate in English. It remained a huge obstacle for me. Fortunately, the requirements for citizenship stated only that an applicant had to have lived legally in the country continuously for at least five years, be "a person of good moral character," support the country and pass a civics test. There was no mention of English fluency. As my friend promised, my application sailed through and I headed to downtown Los Angeles to become a citizen.

A friend accompanied me to the courthouse in Los Angeles on October 21, 1983 for the formal naturalization ceremony. I was nearly forty one. My hands were sweating. I was nervous and excited at the same time. In the office a woman asked me twenty questions. I had studied the civics guides carefully and knew the areas that might be covered. She also had me write one sentence in English. I don't remember which questions she asked, but I recall the sentence. I had practiced writing it out over and over ahead of time! I took a pen and carefully wrote "I take a bus to work from my house."

"Thank you," the woman said with a smile, and directed me to a courtroom for the formal swearing in.

Along with several hundred people from many other countries, I stood before a judge. We raised our right hands and swore the Oath of Allegiance to the United States, repeating each short phrase of it after the judge:

I hereby declare . . . that I absolutely and entirely renounce and abjure all allegiance and fidelity to any foreign prince, potentate, state, or sovereignty of whom or which I have heretofore been a subject or citizen, that I will support and defend the Constitution and laws of the United States of America against all enemies, foreign and domestic; that I will bear true faith and allegiance to the same; that I will bear arms on behalf of the United States when required by the law; that I will perform noncombatant service in the Armed forces of the United States when required by law; that I will perform work of national importance under civilian direction when required by law; and that I take this obligation freely and without any mental reservation or purpose of evasion; so help me God.

I left the building feeling quite emotional. Had my family joined me back in 1974, I thought, we all could have become citizens together. But that had not happened and I had to get on with my life and continue to create my good fortune. The ceremony moved me and filled me with pride. For some time I carried my citizenship certificate with me everywhere I went. Now it is in my safety deposit box, along with my passport, which I applied for right away. And it was all worth it.

Image 7 Lu Chi Fa in 1983

Thirty-three years earlier I had dreamt of riding a dragon in the clouds, high above all my pain and problems. In the last moment before I woke up, the dragon set me down in America. Now I was finally an American citizen, and unlike many of the hopes and dreams I'd had as a child no one could take that away from me—not the cruel "parents" I'd been sold to, not Mean Auntie who'd sent me to do chores when it was time for dinner, not Big Brother who'd beat and robbed me repeatedly. I was free and a citizen of a free country.

Some five years later I heard about a letter President Ronald Reagan read aloud to a group of school children and it moved me to tears. "You can go to live in Japan," a newly naturalized man had written him, "but you cannot become

Japanese. You can go to France to live and not become a Frenchman. You can go to live in Germany or Turkey, and you won't become a German or a Turk. [But]…anybody from any corner of the world can come to America and become an American."

I now possessed all the privileges of an American citizen. I promised myself I would improve my English. I would not shy away from conversations. I would learn two new words every day. I redoubled my commitment to make my life bloom into all that it could possibly become. And that led me into adventures, and risks, that I could not have imagined at the time.

9
SUCCESS: WHEN OPPORTUNITY KNOCKS ANSWER

One Sunday morning an ad in my local Chinese newspaper caught my eye and launched me on my next business venture. A Chinese restaurant in the food court of an upscale shopping mall in Manhattan Beach was for sale. The white real estate agent who'd placed the ad told me about the place in detail, and it sounded perfect. I should have had him handle the purchase, but I felt more comfortable having a Chinese-American realtor to work with. I still feel badly about that.

What motivated me to buy the restaurant? I was afraid of being poor and I needed to prove to myself that I was not a failure. Determined not to repeat the errors of my first restaurant, I planned to learn all I could about how the business was doing and what it would take to make it successful. A friend started negotiations, but we did not let the two brothers who owned the place know who I was.

I visited the mall several times with a retired friend to research the restaurant. We'd sit in a corner of the food court and count how many people entered. At lunchtime we observed an average of ninety-three people in and out every hour. If each person spent about $3.00, I calculated, it could succeed financially. It was a win situation.

I offered $120,000. The owners accepted, then changed their minds and insisted on the full listing price of $150,000. I decided not to let $30,000 kill the deal; the property, I believed, had great potential. So I sold my Santa Ana house and used part of the proceeds as a down payment; I agreed to pay off the remainder within three years. Then I took a step based on the failure of China Diner, one that I've never regretted.

"Look," I said to the owners. "I don't have any experience running a restaurant." Of course this was an exaggeration, but I wanted to avoid mistakes. "For me to learn, I'd be willing to work for free during the forty-five day escrow period."

Surprised, the owners happily agreed to my proposal. It was hard work, but it turned out to be a really good idea. I cleaned the kitchen, washed dishes, chopped food and learned how to make the fifteen items on the menu. I educated myself about every detail of the business. Intent on success, I knew I could rely on no one else.

China Express, my new place, opened in 1984. I was now forty-two years old and resolved that this venture would succeed. And I could see quickly that it would be my path to good fortune. My research had correctly shown that this was a solid investment. In fact, business was so brisk that I paid off the former owners within one year, a full two years ahead of schedule.

Instead of banking the profits, I redecorated and made other changes too. The restaurant had a complicated menu and both drinks and food came in small, medium and large sizes. I realized that having only one size of each item would free up storage space and allow me to take better care of customers. Mall employees didn't have long lunch breaks so they needed fast service! In addition to simplifying the menu, I upgraded some equipment and painted the room with the colors of China—yellow, red and green.

I often ate at a nearby gourmet Chinese restaurant and befriended the owner, Michael Lee. A reserved and somewhat self-important person, I learned quite a bit from him, not about running a restaurant so much as tips for improving the food I served. He loved to pass these along. The suggestion I remember most has to do with broccoli: when cooked for one minute in boiling water with baking soda and a few drops of oil, then drained and rinsed in cold water it will stay green and shiny for two days. Michael enjoyed sharing such cooking tips and I benefitted tremendously.

There has been one amazing, recurring theme in my life. No matter how many people have been mean or cruel or petty to me, and no matter how many times I've tripped or stumbled from my own mistakes, there have always been people who offered me friendship, generosity and love. It's how I survived my childhood, and it's how I overcame the disappointments and setbacks in my adult life.

Making it to the shores of America wasn't the whole story. Living happily here was also an essential piece of my dream. What I realized is that for the most part, we each make our own happiness by the attitudes we adopt and the actions we take. It's a lesson I've learned over and over, and it has served me well.

My happiness took a while to develop at China Express. I had to strengthen my faith in myself first. The major problem stemmed from the fact that the brothers who'd owned the place had gone gambling every afternoon. They would leave the restaurant in the hands of cousins and nephews who prepped, cooked, cleared tables and cared for the customers. Recent immigrants, these relatives had wanted to buy the restaurant but lacked the money to do so. They had even pressured their relatives to rescind the sale to me, but that effort failed. And they weren't used to an on-site boss. Not surprisingly, they hoped my business wouldn't make it.

At first I didn't feel I could fire them. My self-confidence gradually increased. I'd say to myself that I was the owner and the disgruntled workers would be gone soon enough. And that's exactly what happened. When one food server skipped work for two weeks, testing me, I surprised her and let her go. My bartending experience paid off. I also confronted the cooks who had told me repeatedly that I was going to fail. By the end of four and a half months all the original staff had left.

At this point I hired Juan, a tall, stocky Hispanic man, and taught him how to cook the ten basic Chinese dishes we served. We both spoke English poorly, but fortunately I could show him—instead of explain to him—how to prepare each item. And he was a quick learner. At the time a cook's basic salary was $4 an hour. I paid Juan $5.25, and then raised it to $6 because he was so good and I knew he'd help me make money. I gave him a year-end bonus too.

If I put myself into other people's shoes and was unselfish, I came to understand, this would win over the hearts of those who worked for me. Later I brought in a second cook, this man from El Salvador. I realize, looking back, that I didn't know whether either man was legal or not. It just wasn't an issue for me, and it wasn't such a big deal back then.

I also learned from my mistakes. When people asked for half chow mein and half fried rice with their dishes I saw that this slowed down the line. So we asked them to choose one or the other. Although most customers liked the faster service, enough people complained about not having the half and half option that I restored it. Keeping customers happy was important.

After working fourteen hours a day, seven days a week for five years or so I had saved enough money to purchase another place in the food court. My belief then was that such expansion was an important way for me to show that I was successful. This time I ventured outside the cuisine I knew. I bought a small place called Croissant USA. From 10 in the morning until 9 at night it sold croissant sandwiches, soup and salad, coffee, cappuccino, espresso and croissant desserts. I kept the name and the employees and pretty much let them handle the place. This business ran smoothly, and with fewer startup worries than my China Express restaurant.

My success was such that I bought a new home, this one in upscale Manhattan Beach. Complete with four bedrooms, three baths and over 3100 square feet, it perched on a steep slope overlooking the Pacific. A beautiful place, with a lovely courtyard, it expressed how expansive I felt at the time about my good fortune.

10
VISIT BIG SISTER

I was doing so well by 1986 that I decided to visit Big Sister in China. For some time I'd wanted to see her. She had rescued me from the horrible abusive "parents" I'd been sold to, and done what she could to protect me as a child. She'd also given me advice that I never forgot. "These cruel things happening to you will pass," she'd said, "and getting through them will make you strong." And they had.

I prided myself on all that I had done and wanted Big Sister to know about my good fortune. But returning to the country I'd escaped from in 1951 worried me. The memories of that hazardous time frightened me. And I was well aware of the many changes that had taken place in China. Had it not been for Big Sister, I would not have considered going back.

My sister had lived in Shanghai when I was seven, working as a maid for a well-to-do couple. I remembered the address and phone number of the home where she'd worked and I recalled that she had lived nearby. The Chinese consulate in Washington, D.C. provided me with her current address and I wrote her, including pictures and telling her that I wanted to visit. She wrote back, sounding excited but a bit distant. I planned my trip, worried because I knew she was still married to Chi Haw, the man who had hated me because I wasn't *his* son. Yet it felt important to do this. If not now, I said to myself, when? My business obligations meant I couldn't be there long. In fact, I'd have only seventy-two hours in China itself.

In Shanghai I hired a taxi driver and we eventually found Big Sister's building on a narrow alley in a poor neighborhood. To me it looked as if I was stepping back in time, or into a war zone. Near her building I saw people filling buckets of water, making me think that the area lacked indoor plumbing. As I stood there pondering this, a woman walked past me and into the building. I just knew that it was my sister.

Before I headed after her, I told my driver to come get me in forty-five minutes. I feared my reunion wouldn't go well because of Chi Haw. My sister opened the door of their apartment, but at first said nothing. She didn't seem to recognize me. I'd been seven when she last saw me. After a moment of awkward silence a woman who turned out to be her youngest daughter, my cousin I realized, put her hand on Big Sister's shoulder.

"Ma," she said, "this is your brother. Chi Fa has come from the United States of America to visit you."

Big Sister seemed to wake up. Once she understood who I was, we fell into each other's arms. She was sixty-four now, twenty years older than me, looked even more elderly and seemed to be in poor health. "My little Chi Fa," she said, over and over as we hugged. "I cannot believe it is you."

"Big Sister," I told her, "I have so much to share with you."

She didn't invite me into her apartment, which I saw was tiny. Instead, we gathered on the sidewalk in front of the building— Big Sister, her youngest daughter and husband and their child. We chatted in a general way, until my driver showed up. It was just as well, as Big Sister said that Chi Haw would be returning shortly and I had no desire to encounter him.

Back at the hotel I thought about how my sister lived. It shocked and depressed me. Her tiny apartment, what I'd seen of it when I peeked inside, could not have been much more than one hundred fifty square feet, hardly larger than my bathroom at home. The main room had a table and four stools. Narrow stairs on one side of the room, my cousin later told me, led to a space where Big Sister and Chi Haw shared a sleeping platform with another couple. There a curtain down the middle provided the only privacy. I suspected they lived hand to mouth, as I had as a child, still worried about where their next meal would come from. Of course this made me acutely conscious of my own quite different situation back in Orange County. The contrast, I thought, was unimaginable.

On the second day in Shanghai my driver took me to nearby Taihu Lake, the third largest freshwater lake in China. Wherever we went young people seemed to know, probably because of my clothing and haircut, that I was a foreigner. They bombarded me with questions. How did I get to the United

States? Did I own my own home? Was there discrimination there? I avoided discussing politics as I did not want to cause any problems, for them or me.

When it was time for lunch I invited my driver to join me at a restaurant overlooking the beautiful lake. He was hesitant at first, but then we had a scrumptious meal and talked in generalities about nonpolitical topics. A seemingly cautious man, he provided no information about himself. In retrospect, I wish I'd gotten to know him better and learned about his life.

The service was quite different from restaurants in many other countries, and as a restaurant owner I of course noticed it. The waiters, all clad in blue Mao outfits, were cold and distant. They got impatient if you asked a question and lacked any sense of courtesy. They seemed to have no need to please customers, and I wondered if that was because they received the same pay no matter how hard they worked. Tipping wasn't part of the culture.

After we finished eating, we headed back into the city to see Big Sister. When I knocked on the front door of the dilapidated place where they lived, no one answered. I kept knocking and a window on the second floor opened. An old man I recognized as Chi Haw looked down at me, frowned and then closed the window. I remembered how nasty he'd been to me all those years ago, and I'd like to think maybe he closed the window because he carried guilt or shame from his actions.

Still, I assumed that he would come down to open the door. So I waited and waited. But he never appeared. In time a woman opened the door and told me that Big Sister had already headed toward my hotel. That's where my taxi driver and I found her. My beloved Shiow Jen, clad in a padded Mao outfit, stood outside the entry looking forlorn. The hotel doorman hadn't let her wait inside. I explained that she was my sister. He didn't believe me at first, but I assured him she was not an outsider and in time he let us both enter.

When she saw my room, my sister held her hand to her mouth and gasped. "It's like a palace," she said. "So big, so clean." She tested the bed. "Oh my," she said. "So soft."

I smiled, thinking that in reality the room was only slightly better than what you'd find in some budget motel in the States. This was another of those small moments that made me realize how fortunate I was. "Let me get us something to drink," I said, and brought back two Cokes.

Big Sister took a sip, frowned and shook her head. "This tastes like medicine."

We had such a short time together and I still had so much to tell her. I wanted our talk to be positive and not dwell on the hardships of the past. We held hands and I told her of my success in America. I was so proud of what I'd done that I wanted her to know how important what she'd told me decades before had been to me. She'd said I was a strong person and that difficulty would educate me. I told her how I'd often thought of what she'd said, and how her words had helped me through rough times.

She smiled and shook her head. "You own a restaurant. My little Chi Fa. Ha. I knew you would find good fortune."

Eventually Big Sister told me how hard her life had been. She and Chi Haw twice had spent long stints at separate labor "re-education" camps during the Cultural Revolution, although why, she said, was unclear. Perhaps, I thought, it was because back in the day Chi Haw had inherited considerable land and was a landowner. After release, in any case, they'd reunited and continued to live in poverty.

She seemed nervous as we headed back to her apartment and kept glancing at my driver, apparently fearful of what he might hear. So we said little. We dropped her off and I said we would pick her up the next day, the last day of my visit, for a lunch given by her youngest daughter.

It was a big meal. Once more Chi Haw wasn't there, which made things easier. We ate course after course of specially prepared foods, but didn't talk about our past. In the Chinese culture it's considered more important to treat all visitors well—even long-lost family—rather than to have long, deep conversations. Also, I think my relatives wanted to avoid any talk that government agents might view as disloyal. One could not be too careful seemed to be the attitude.

On the way back to my hotel we dropped off Big Sister. Once at the hotel I paid my driver, double the set amount. He turned to me with a huge smile.

"My boss told me to keep an eye on you," he confessed. "But when I saw you reunite with your sister that touched me. I will report nothing."

Perhaps the fact that I'd paid him so much may have affected him too, I thought. "Thank you, thank you," I said, wondering what he could possibly have reported. I had suspected that Chinese intelligence might have been interested in my visit and I was glad that I'd avoided discussing politics with anyone.

When my plane took off from Shanghai, I wept. Big Sister and I came from the same parents, but I had a beautiful life in the U.S. I had food, money in the bank, easy access to medical care and, most important, freedom. She had none of these things. She hadn't been able to take me in when I was a child, but she had done her best and she had always loved me. If she had been a modern Chinese woman she could have spoken up to Chi Haw. But back then, in China and in Taiwan also, women were second-class citizens. They didn't have the same rights as men.

I also thought about Chi Haw. He could have acted differently when I'd been a child. He and my sister had daughters, and instead of being jealous of my presence he could have welcomed me as his son. I could have belonged to their family, and not been forced to hide in a dark and airless shed because a grown man was jealous of me. I would not have been sent away to beg and starve.

Every now and then, even today, this sadness rises up in me. I feel it but push through and return to the present. The present is far more important to me than the past.

When I arrived back in America, I sent Big Sister money. The Chinese government converted it into something like a pre-paid credit card that allowed her to shop in a "Friendship" store. There she could buy Western food, clothing and even luxuries. She apparently feared it could be a ruse to determine her loyalty and subject her to "re-education," however, so she never used that card or received the comforts it would have bought her. First her husband, then the government had ground down all her fierceness and courage. Long gone was the brave woman who'd used anger, threats and guile to free me from bondage to my cruel adoptive parents.

In the spring of the following year, I got news that Big Sister had died. Part of my child-heart died with her.

11
ADAPT TO THE UNEXPECTED

I returned from China tired, grateful and overconfident about my successes. My business dreams caused me to make a big mistake. I believed I was smart and intelligent, yet what I did next was neither. I split my energies even further, and in 1988 bought a third food-court restaurant.

Au Chocolate was a kiosk with a sink, espresso machine and gourmet chocolates. The concept was good, especially for upscale Manhattan Beach, but this time I hadn't done my market research. There was a See's Candies store within a block of the mall. I just never had seen it because I'd always been too busy to explore the town! See's had cornered the chocolate business with low prices and a strong reputation. I couldn't compete with them and my classy little Au chocolate kiosk didn't do well.

This situation reminded me of an old Chinese proverb: "There are no mistakes, only lessons." But what were the lessons? That's the question I needed to ask, and answer. By this time I had been living for several years in a beautiful gated community in Manhattan Beach. I'd believed that being in a "white" area would improve my language skills, especially the idioms that I found so hard to understand and the many exceptions to the rules of grammar. That hadn't happened; I just worked too many hours to socialize much with neighbors. Still, the way that you know if you've really learned another language is when you start to think in it. And by this time, to my amazement, I had actually begun to do that.

But my ability with the English language actually wasn't the lesson I needed to examine. The truth, I had to admit, was that my two successful businesses and one flagging chocolate kiosk had not come easily. In my aggressive pursuit of success I had overextended myself and was *totally* exhausted, physically and mentally. I'd been working non-stop for seven years. In reality, I'd been working without a break since I was four years old. I felt stressed and had gotten too thin. Now in my mid-forties I had a twenty-eight inch waist, below normal for a man my height, no matter how much American culture admires slimness. If I kept going at this pace, I fretted, my health would decline quickly.

I decided that this was a sign and that I needed to listen to my body and trust my urgent need to get away. I put all three businesses on the market, hoping to sell quickly. Croissant USA and China Express both did, and for a good price. I had offered China Express to a restaurant owner I knew, but he'd declined and bought another place closer to the ocean in Manhattan Beach. As it turned out, he had to pour a lot of money into remodeling it, and then it failed. He was, I concluded, a smart man, but not wise. My wisdom was to basically give away the kiosk. I was *delighted* to get rid of it! I now felt free from the self-inflected pressures of my own success.

To start my long period of planned rest, I enlisted Bob, an old friend, to accompany me on a trip. He knew a professor of Russian literature who, with his Russian wife, regularly escorted visits to the Soviet Union. Having a knowledgeable guide appealed to me, although the prospect of going to a Communist country triggered memories of my experiences in China. But I was so exhausted that I just wanted to get away. The opportunity was there and I seized it.

In Moscow security was tight, the culture militaristic and controlling. Armed soldiers seemed to be everywhere, probably because of the political unrest at the time. I wasn't really aware of that as much as of the poorness of the country. That was very evident when I visited a farmers market and saw how little was available. This reinforced my gratitude for being where I was.

St. Petersburg, the former capital of Imperial Russia, seemed like a movie set strewn with empty palaces and fabulous old churches. The summer and winter palaces displayed the wealth and gaudy extravagance of the czars, a stunning contrast to the evident poverty of the country. That contrast wasn't the only thing I noticed. Our Russian tour guide couldn't interpret any of the frescoes at the churches since he'd never learned about religion.

I did my part contributing to the economy by purchasing a big fur hat, and a massage. The woman who worked on me was a giant—fully six feet tall, with huge hands. She was not gentle. "Please," I said, "that's enough. I'll pay you to stop." But she didn't. She grunted and kept on. Maybe I was having a classic Russian experience.

We traveled home by way of Berlin, and I again thought about what I'd seen in the Soviet Union. The hotel where we stayed served a breakfast which included, among other things, a great variety of potatoes and sausages. The sheer volume of food stood in dramatic contrast to what had been available in Moscow and St. Petersburg.

While here we visited the wall which had once separated East and West Berlin. For a small price I rented a sledge hammer from an enterprising kid and knocked off a piece of the now-crumbling wall as souvenir of democracy winning out over Communism. I still have the chunk of concrete. Given my own experiences, it means a lot to me.

12
FINDING HOME

I returned to the U.S. filled with gratitude for the life I'd created, but still eager to do more. So my good friend Bob and I drove north along the California coast, enjoying the ocean views and the lack of responsibility. We spent the night at the quaint fishing-tourism-and-retirement town of Morro Bay, home to nine thousand souls. I had visited there a couple of times before and liked it.

A quiet and peaceful place most of the year, Morro Bay had a busy summer season with visitors streaming in from Los Angeles and the Central Valley. It boasted a movie theater with one screen, a small but treacherous harbor and a busy waterfront where you could hear sea lions barking as you strolled by the cute shops and restaurants. Sea otters floated in clusters at the foot of giant Morro Rock while sea lions poked their whiskery noses out of the water and birds chatted noisily. The town hosted an annual festival for birders and once-endangered peregrine falcons nested high on Morro Rock.

It seemed like the perfect place for me to slow down for a while, or for good. I had vowed never again to let business wear me out. There was just one snag. I couldn't escape my own nature. We stopped at Century 21 on Morro Bay Boulevard and talked to a realtor.

"I'm looking for a property that will give a good return," I told her, and briefly explained my situation. "I'm really tired and I don't want a place I have to be busy with."

She smiled and nodded. Bob stood by patiently, shaking his head as the realtor discussed different properties. Then the three of us spent the day looking at office buildings, motels and apartment houses. I knew that I wanted to find a way to make good use of the money from the sale of my businesses without getting too personally involved. Whatever we looked at, however, left me cold and feeling empty inside. Nothing seemed really right.

I think fortune, "good fortune" as Big Sister would say, had something else in mind for me. That evening the realtor called to tell me that a small home-style breakfast and lunch restaurant just off the waterfront had come on the market. The next morning Bob and I went to take a look at The Coffee Pot. It was the weekend and there was a crowd waiting outside to get in.

As I watched the people in line, many of whom seemed to know each other, I knew that buying the place would be a challenge, and a big risk. I'd never owned a business serving American food. I knew nothing about it! I had never cooked a

Denver omelet or made waffles, flipped burgers, prepared "French" fries or . . . you get the picture. In fact I'd never *cooked* American food, not even for myself. And of course there were a certain irony about this, given my disastrous first experiment with the beverage coffee decades earlier.

I had other qualms as well. Actually warning bells went off in my head. After all, it was 1990, I was forty-nine and exhausted. I had sold my businesses and hoped to find an investment that would generate income without lots of effort. I needed to rest, yet here I was thinking about buying an active business which handled a cuisine I had no experience with. My China Diner and Au Chocolat failures had taught me the importance of doing careful research before venturing into a new business. Yet despite the fatigue and lack of careful research I found myself tempted to plunge into a new restaurant.

For a couple of weeks I watched The Coffee Pot from our rented place above the Embarcadero. And what I saw reinforced my gut feeling that the place could be a winner. It had a steady flow of customers, every day. Despite my fatigue and resolve not to get directly involved in another restaurant, I set aside all the logical reservations.

The Coffee Pot just felt right. Maybe my experiences of working all my life had something to do with it. Maybe I'd lost the ability to do nothing. Maybe working had become my identity and how I defined my own sense of self-worth. Maybe it was simply that it appeared comfortable to me because it was in a familiar line of business. I can't say for sure.

In any case, The Coffee Pot struck me as being a friendly place, a home at last; it *felt* right. It was at the quiet end of the Embarcadero, almost at the water's edge. The décor was simple. Small tables filled the dining room and colorful coffee pots graced shelves. The food was straightforward and it was homey and filled with people who seemed to be enjoying the food and themselves.

"It's quite popular with locals and visitors," the realtor told me, confirming what my own observations had suggested. "A lot of folks come back regularly."

I took this as a good sign. Bob agreed. In fact, he stopped worrying and no longer discouraged me from buying another restaurant. I decided to go for it. The quality and location of the business impressed Bob so much that he set aside his own hesitations, and asked if he could go in with me as a silent partner. I agreed and we put in our offer, which the owners accepted immediately!

Then I made a familiar deal. I'd work for free during the escrow period if they taught me how to cook the American food on the menu and show me whatever else I needed to know about the restaurant. Less than two months to learn everything? This was no food court stall. This was a busy, sit-down restaurant with a big menu and lots of hungry customers, many of whom hadn't had their coffee yet. And it was a cuisine I knew nothing about.

At China Express there had been nearby Chinese restaurateurs I could talk with. In Morro Bay there were a few other Chinese, but not in restaurants like the one I was buying. One consolation: American food is less complicated to prepare than Chinese. Okay, I thought, I've survived tougher situations. I can do this.

Before the sale closed I worked seven days a week for eight to ten hours a day, with only one lunch break daily. This was not the rest I'd told myself I needed, and the owners, it turned out, were not that easy to work with. But I'd faced difficulties before and determined to persist. Rather than complain or be upset, I focused on the end goal. In forty five days I would be my own boss in an already going concern that clearly was a good investment.

By the time escrow closed I had learned the basics of cooking the American dishes and even practical subtleties such as how to balance the three different chemicals used in the dishwasher. It took me two years to master everything involved with the business, including the foods on the menu.

Tea remained my non-alcoholic drink of choice, but since coffee was in the name of my new restaurant I decided to learn more about the beverage. I'd acquired a taste for coffee over the years, preferred blends from South America, and had enough experience to know when it was too weak or had been brewed hours before. Beyond that, I knew little. So I did some research.

I found out that the process begins with coffee beans harvested from either Coffea arabica or Coffea canephora plants which grow mainly in areas near the equator. Each plant yields beans with different characteristics once they are dried, roasted and ground. Sixty percent of annual production is Coffea arabica, also known as Arabian Coffee. Coffea robusta, comes from the other plant, is lower in acidity and higher in bitterness and used mainly in instant coffee and espresso. About one-third of all the coffee in the world comes from Brazil, but Vietnam is the major producer of robusta. That surprised me.

Changing vendors and getting a better quality of coffee was just one of the small improvements I made right away. Another was to put benches and a commercial coffee urn out front. When people had to wait for a table, I took them cups of coffee and chatted with them.

Morro Bay gets very busy in the spring and summer. Birders, retirees and families on vacation from the intense heat of the Central Valley flock to our more temperate coastal climate. And often they return to The Coffee Pot. Sometimes I'd sit with them for a while. I got to know their names, their families and their stories.

Pretty soon I noticed that I had begun to see my guests and employees as family. Soon some of them started thinking of me as family too and wrote me letters during the off-season winter months.

Looking back, I don't think it's a coincidence that I ended up running businesses where I was responsible for and took great pleasure in feeding people. Being hungry, even starving, shaped my childhood. That experience made me relish food, and it taught me too the value of kindness. I'd ventured into the restaurant business with China Diner and then China Express. Now I had something even better to offer.

13

BE KIND

In my first year at The Coffee Pot I did my best to ensure that customers were well treated and well fed. I focused on customer service and quality food, as well as food presentation. As a bus boy at the officers' club in Taiwan decades earlier I'd learned how important it was to attract people's eyes before their stomach. To my great delight, the business went well at first, and then it got better and better.

Along with Bob and another friend who came up from Los Angeles to give me support, I rented the lower part of a house near the restaurant. I decided to keep my house in Manhattan Beach temporarily, but after four months leased it furnished. I knew I'd made the right decision and landed in the right place.

Confident about my choices, I bought a house near the Morro Bay golf course. It had one thousand square feet, an ocean view and a mother-in-law unit in the backyard. It was less than a mile from the restaurant and the neighbors were friendly. It even turned out that the town's mayor, Bill Yates, lived right next door. Surely this was a good sign, evidence of my good fortune.

I kept The Coffee Pot open seven days a week from 7 a.m. to 2 p.m., serving breakfast and lunch. Most of the menu items were American dishes: corned beef hash, Belgian waffles, a variety of omelets, honey-smoked bacon, fish and chips, clam chowder, hamburgers and many different sandwiches. I changed the previous owner's menu slowly, well aware of the importance of getting to know my customers first. After all, many of them had been coming to The Coffee Pot longer than I had been.

From the start I had regular customers who came in more than once a week, and there were only a few disgruntled people. The one I remember most clearly shouted: "What do you know about American food? You won't last more than six months!" I never did figure out what set him off, but happily he was the exception. And years later I saw that same man, and politely told him that I still owned The Coffee Pot.

Staffing the restaurant didn't go smoothly at first. Originally there were nineteen part-timers, most of them related to the former owner. They worked short shifts, some only two hours! This made the payroll too big and scheduling clumsy, at best. Whenever one of these folks left, I didn't replace them. I did fire one fellow. When he burned a coffee roll, dumped it and made another, he went. I couldn't afford such waste. The staff gradually shrank to a reasonable size.

For the first year I was at The Coffee Pot all the time. I had learned that if you own a restaurant and aren't there to manage the place, you will lose money. Other things fell into place over time. I bought all my food and restaurant supplies from just a couple of vendors. I focused on customer service, cleanliness and quality food such as thick, center-cut smoked bacon. I made only small modifications to the dining room, keeping the country-kitchen look but replacing chairs, tables and mugs. I didn't make any significant profit until the third year.

When necessary, I continued to make small changes. For instance, we used to serve a giant cinnamon roll that was quite popular. But one day back in the '90s I watched a group of four ladies order the roll, split it four ways and ask several times for more butter and lemon slices for their water. They stayed for two hours, and we brought in just $1.75. I immediately took the famous cinnamon roll off the menu. We couldn't afford it! Some people criticized me, but I kept doing what was right for the business. The restaurant, I understood, was not a charity and I could not let people take advantage of me.

One fellow tried to do that. He was a nasty man with a loud voice who insisted on paying half price for things. That was obnoxious enough, but he also didn't bathe regularly. He smelled. To top it off, he wouldn't talk to me directly. Since it was still early in my ownership of The Coffee Pot, I was hesitant to act quickly. But after a while I saw that he disturbed other customers too. When he sat down people close by moved to a different table. I gritted my teeth and reminded myself that my bartending experience would come in handy. I knew how to 86 people.

I stood in front of him and said "I want you out of here." He looked puzzled, frowned and I repeated what I'd said. After several minutes, he pushed back his plate, grumbled about lousy service and food and left. To my surprise the other customers applauded. My courage to face him directly made me proud.

Another early challenge occurred when a man who must have weighed over 300 pounds came into the restaurant. I knew most of the chairs could not support him, so when he chose a table I exchanged his chair for one that I knew could.

"Are you telling me I'm fat," he yelled.

I swallowed, thought fast and said "No, I'm just concerned about your safety." I was too green then to tell him my opinion, and I'm sorry he didn't understand that I wanted to protect him from a fall. Since he cursed at me, something he did not need to do, it's unlikely that he believed what I'd said. After that incident I upgraded all the chairs. Today I've gained enough assurance so that I would say "Yes, you're too fat."

After two years there was no question that I'd found my right place. The business was doing well and I liked where I was. So I sold my Manhattan Beach house and planned to buy a bigger place near The Coffee Pot. That idea changed when I attended an open house in Los Osos. It's a small town six miles south of Morro Bay, across the beautiful estuary where egrets fish in the shallow waters, kayakers paddle among the reeds and great blue herons nest in the fragrant eucalyptus trees.

The 3,300 square foot house high on a hillside above the town amazed me, for it provided a magnificent view of the ocean, estuary, Morro Rock and the coastline beyond it. It had three bedrooms, two and a half baths, a formal dining room, a living room, a sunroom and a workshop. There was a patio in the rear and deer drifted through the backyard. The house was too good to pass up.

Are you wondering why I talk about this property in such detail? Maybe it's not as interesting to you as it was to me. Remember, I never had a home of my own as a child. I have no fond memories of the bed where I slept or of the kitchen where my family gathered to eat meals. I bounced from house to shack to house, from relative to stranger to relative, and then to refugee camps and later to a one-room shack on a hillside.

I guess the many homes I have created for myself as an adult hold a fascination for me that endures to this day because of that background. Later, as I tell you about the other homes I bought and built, and lost, I hope you'll understand how deeply important each one was to me. They were all a part of my American dream, my good fortune, though I hadn't realized it when I was younger. To me they represented safety, security and proof of success in my new country.

As it turned out, buying such a big place was a good move. The next year I would need room for my older son Jason, and less than a year later for my younger son Kevin.

14

LOVE YOUR FAMILY—AND
SET LIMITS!

Jason arrived in 1993, not long after he'd completed his military service in Taiwan. I hadn't seen him for over a decade. He was twenty-five now, close to the age I'd been when I came to the United States, and he arrived with much the same idea as I'd had when I immigrated. He wanted to have a better future. He seemed much taller than I remembered. A sharp dresser, he'd been a model for a time in Taiwan. Since I was an American citizen he received his green card quickly, so he had none of the issues I'd faced at the outset. For me though it was a challenge.

In China a good father provides for his children, ensures they are educated and trains them in the Chinese value of filial piety. I had no grounding in that Confucian tradition. My father had died when I was three. My Big Sister's husband, my adoptive father and my Big Brother had all been cruel to me. And I'd been with my sons only a few years. I had visited them in Taiwan several times after Vivian decided not to join me in the U.S., but we were not close and although I was proud of Jason the reunion was awkward.

My son lived in the granny unit in my backyard so he had his own place and privacy. And Jason did something I'd been unable to do when I first arrived because my work schedule changed so often. He enrolled in a course to study English as a second language at the nearby community college. We always ate dinner and Sunday brunch together, but my long hours at The Coffee Pot limited the time I could spend with him otherwise.

When we could, we sat on the front patio, looked at the ocean and found things to talk about. He told me about his two compulsory years in the military and working as a model and a model's agent. Mostly he spent his time learning English so he could get a good job and stay in America. But he had difficulty adjusting to the situation in San Luis Obispo County. Local transportation and cultural activities paled compared to Taiwan, and he had difficulty with the food as well.

Less than a year later, Kevin, now twenty-five, joined us. Quite thin, he had finished his military service too and worked several different jobs in Taiwan. He moved into the granny unit with his brother and like him took English classes. The three of us ate together often and were companionable, but somewhat distant. I didn't know how to give them fatherly affection the way an American father would, so it felt to me as if I wasn't quite getting it.

Soon Jason and Kevin made friends at school. They spent a lot of time on the phone with them. Sometimes they met their buddies at coffee shops or at their homes in Morro Bay or the nearby college town of San Luis Obispo. I'd drive them there and their friends would bring them home. Once they got their driver's licenses they took off on their own in the evening using my car.

When they found an apartment in San Luis Obispo to share with a friend I agreed to pay their share of the rent. That felt like the right thing to do. Although I wanted them to learn how to be independent, I didn't want to be too hard on them. Besides, they were still taking their English classes.

Unfortunately, I miscalculated how my sons would react to not having their other living expenses taken care of. They used the spending money I gave them to buy cigarettes and fancy sunglasses. In a few days the money would be gone and they'd ask for more. A Chinese parent would have given them everything they wanted, but I would not. They resented this and complained that I'd become too Americanized.

Once my sons finished their first level English classes they headed three hours north to San Jose, in the heart of Silicon Valley. I gave them seed money and purchased a small mobile home for them. "You're on your own now," I told them. "It's time you start to create your own good fortune."

Although it was hard for me to do this, I wanted them to be successful adults, able to support themselves and make their own lives. "This is America, not China," I said. "You can't rely on someone else." They were angry with me for some time.

Often it felt as if they hated me, but I knew I was doing the right thing for them.

Jason got a job as a sushi chef in a Japanese restaurant right away. Kevin worked in a fancy Chinese restaurant. When things cooled down between us, I'd visit them in San Jose. On hot days we'd sit by the swimming pool and they'd talk about their lives. We'd marvel at the three of us being together in America. I was slowly learning how to be a father and they were learning how to be grownups. I don't recall that there was any talk about them staying in the U.S. They had permanent green cards, so it just wasn't an issue.

15
SPEAK YOUR TRUTH

Late in the nineties something happened that would help me deal with my horrible childhood, although I did not know that at the time. At a fourth of July party in 1999 I met Karen Grencik, a local woman starting a literary agency. She'd heard about my impoverished youth and escape from China and thought it would make a wonderful book for children. At the time her idea puzzled me and I had no idea how profoundly her proposal would change my life.

"I never finished grade school," I said. "How could I write such a book?"

No, Karen explained, she'd take down my story and then have an experienced writer put the words on paper, edit them and shape a book aimed at children. This seemed too good to be true, but Karen assured me that my story was worth telling.

"Chi Fa, it's a tale that needs to be told. You survived a horrendous childhood, and look at you today."

Karen, it turned out, was a former court reporter skilled at recording talks. She brought her stenotype machine to my place and we met a number of times so she could record my story from childhood until I came to the United States. Once she was satisfied that she had everything, she held a lunch and invited eight writers who she thought might be interested in turning my story into a book. Becky White, a successful author of books for children, wanted to do the project, so Karen suggested that she write a couple of chapters and show them to me. When I saw the results, I was overwhelmed.

It took Becky about a year to complete the final manuscript, and she marvelously captured my childhood thoughts, trials and feelings. Going over the final manuscript with her brought tears to my eyes. She'd done such a wonderful job that it took my breath away.

Karen worked hard and eventually placed the manuscript with Holiday House. When it published ***Double Luck: Memoirs of a Chinese Orphan*** in 2001, I was humbled, grateful and excited all at once.

John Briggs, the President of Holiday House, sent a marvelous letter: "First it was Double Luck. Now it is Double Happiness. And my fortune cookie . . . reads, 'You are lucky. Good Fortune will find you.'" It surely did, for the next year the book won a gold award from the Parents' Choice Foundation.

My friend Azul Hull taught English at Xi'an International Studies University in China, and donated copies there and at several other schools. Over the years I've sent copies to other Chinese libraries. The fact that this has been possible says a lot about how much that country has changed.

Image 8 Azul Hull and Ann Zheng

Meanwhile, the book kept selling. In 2005 it was still the number one best seller in the area. All this of course made my good fortune almost more than I could imagine.

Thanks to this award and the publicity that came with it, a friend told me that I was now the second most famous resident of Morro Bay. "Jack LaLanne, the health food and exercise guru, is number one," he said with a big smile. "And you're right behind him." Although I didn't think of myself that way, news about the book and award attracted attention; local elementary and junior high schools, libraries, book clubs and Rotary clubs in the area invited me to give talks about my experiences as a child.

Image 9 Interviewed in 2002, Lu Chi Explained the need to push away problems

Public speaking wasn't something I had any skill at. I'm a people person and always have been, but I had never spoken to groups before and was shy about doing that. So, although my recollections generated a lot of interest, the early talks were difficult. My first speaking date was to a group of women at the local Catholic Church. I was nervous, not sure how to start or how to end. But people were kind. And one lady suggested something that served me well. "Gordon," she said, "you don't have to tell the whole book." I took that advice.

Despite my lack of polish early on, there were many good moments. I especially remember one talk to a group of about one hundred men at a local inn. I was still learning how to express myself, but when I finished they gave me a standing round of applause. It amazed and overwhelmed me. I was so emotional that after the event I drove to the nearby beautiful Montana de Oro State Park and wept. As I stood there overlooking the Pacific, I remembered my childhood when I'd had nothing and been so hungry, starved for affection and cruelly treated. And here I was, now middle-aged, with love coming to me from so many directions.

It took three or four years to get comfortable with telling my story in public. In time I learned how to choose the right words for different audiences, how not to get bogged down in details and how to hold the attention of the audience. It was a process, and every talk got a little better. What didn't change was that these talks always brought back a flush of memories.

No matter how many times I spoke, this was the case, even after several years. Although I became far more comfortable speaking in front of people, I remember clearly how one day after a talk I went a nearby park, stood in a grove of trees and cried aloud for having been born such a nothing, being so uneducated and unwanted. Now people asked me to share my wisdom with young people. I felt deeply humbled and at the same time grateful for the experience.

I had promised myself long ago that someday I'd help other children so that they would not have the kind of experiences I had had. Talking to kids in schools and libraries was a step toward using the horrible memories of my childhood in a positive way.

After a while word of my story spread beyond our local area. I kept copies of my book at The Coffee Pot and many customers who ate there took copies home. One family found **Double Luck** at a used book store and read it aloud on the trip back to Porterville in California's San Joaquin Valley. It turned out that Professor Ted Wise taught English at Porterville College. A warm, outgoing and helpful man, he adopted the book as required reading in one of his classes and then invited me to speak. His charming wife and daughter were educators too, and they spread the word in the area. Soon I received invitations to talk to classes at more distant middle schools and other two-year colleges in California's financially strapped Central Valley.

Telling my story to young kids touched me deeply. Although California's Central Valley provides a third of all the produce in the U.S., it is one of the poorest regions in the country. The mostly Mexican and Mexican-American farm workers often lack much education. I felt that the opportunity to speak to their children was important, because in many ways my impoverished childhood had some similarities to theirs. I could show them that growing up with poverty and harsh conditions need not prevent success as an adult.

Each class I visited had read my book beforehand; teachers had read it to the youngest students. In their eyes I was famous, a real live author. Kids would shout out that I had arrived and rush down the hall to greet me. Primarily from farm-worker families with rough lives, they identified with my childhood and the tale of broken families and the struggle to make ends meet. They felt I was one of them.

"You hit them where they live," one teacher told me later. This touched me deeply. Sharing my hardships and grief released some of the pain I still carried, and more important hopefully relieved some of theirs as well. And that is why I've returned to these schools year after year. There are always young people I want to get my message across to.

Typically I charged the schools and other groups for these talks. Then I donated a large part of the proceeds to libraries and reading groups to buy books. Eventually I funded two scholarships at Porterville College. One, an endowed scholarship, continues in perpetuity. The other is an annual scholarship awarded when donations to it reach $500 in a given year. This was a way of saying thank you to Ted Wise, who has retired and now lives in nearby Los Osos. Ted teaches via the internet and still uses my book as required reading.

Sometimes all this amazes me. I lack much education and yet am valued enough to speak to students at various levels. Once when a group of college students visited The Coffee Pot a young woman asked me how much education I'd had as a child. I turned toward a wall and stifled my tears. In all my talks I'd never admitted how little education I'd had. I took a deep breath and turned back to her. In truth, I confessed, I never finished second grade. I felt better inside after saying that.

I kept meeting people who disagreed with my lowly self-assessment. In 2005 Kamala Carlson, a Professor of English at Taft College in the far southwest corner of the Central Valley, visited The Coffee Pot. A friend had read ***Double Luck*** and recommended that she incorporate it into one of her classes. For more than eleven years now I've been visiting Kamala's classes, telling my story and answering questions. The students read my book beforehand and connect with my experience, guided by a detailed set of questions Kamala gives them. To top it off, she arranges to have egg rolls and pot stickers provided.

In 2007 life provided another test for my growing sense of self-worth. Connie Hanretty Church called to say she had read ***Double Luck*** in her book club. My story had deeply touched the members, all women with young children. It turned out that Connie taught psychology and child development at California Polytechnic State University in nearby San Luis Obispo. She wanted to include my book as required reading in a class on "Conflict Resolution: Violent and Non-Violent" and asked if I would tell my story to her class.

Her request intimidated me. Until then I'd been talking to kids in elementary grades, high schools and community colleges. Despite my hesitation and concerns, I'd finally gotten used to being someone worth listening to. But Cal Poly was a four-year university. Students were well-educated and well-to-do, members of America's privileged class. What could I teach them? In China education is highly valued and teachers have a high status. Surely the idea that her ragged, barefoot, hungry and unschooled little Chi Fa was going to talk at an elite university would amaze Big Sister.

Despite my nervousness all went well, and Connie then asked me to speak at her class on child abuse. This puzzled me. I knew the term in a general way, but had never thought of what happened to me as "child abuse." My treatment when I was little was just how things were. There was no name for it. It was simply my life.

I ended up talking to Connie's classes year after year. Her praise helped me gradually overcome my sense of unworthiness. The book and talks, she assured me, taught students about resiliency and hopefulness. "What you give them," she said, "trumps ordinary academic education. It's not even comparable." Student reactions—from hugs to laudatory words—reinforced this message. Still, I really don't know what to do with all the praise heaped on me. I am humbled and grateful, and often reminded that I needed those hugs and kind words as a kid.

16
A THIRST FOR ADVENTURE

The talks I gave and the success of The Coffee Pot boosted my confidence and sense of self-worth. I had indeed created good fortune. That feeling deepened in 2006 when my son Kevin and his wife Sophie, who both had experience in the restaurant business, moved from San Jose and bought The China Dragon restaurant in North Morro Bay. I was thrilled to have them near me, although I was a little anxious. I hoped they were serious and that they would create their own good fortune, instead of doing what I'd seen so many people do—wait for it to arrive.

I need not have worried. Although I helped them get set up, encouraged my customers to go there and lent them my cook for a while, their hard work molded their business success. Soon they had regular customers and a thriving business. It made me proud.

About this same time my silent partner Bob moved out of the area. I bought out his share but kept a painting he'd done hanging in the restaurant, a reminder of his role in making The Coffee Pot succeed. A very particular man, he'd helped with such details as how to set the tables properly. Some people hadn't liked his insistence on how to do things they considered unimportant, but his assistance had been invaluable and helped make The Coffee Pot a better restaurant. Among other things he had handled licenses, relations with government agencies and health inspections, tasks I was happy to turn over.

Not long after this my personal assistant quit. At a July 4th celebration in Shell Beach I met Milt Carrigan, a highly educated man (Yale and Harvard) and he started helping me with correspondence about speaking engagements. Over the years since 2005 he has helped with various issues at the restaurant as well. He's become a close friend.

Having Sophie and Kevin nearby helped too. Sophie handled the business side of their restaurant, and I knew I could rely on her to fill in for me from time to time. With The Coffee Pot running smoothly, I could continue to travel when I wanted to without having to leave my beloved business in the hands of the wait staff. They already had their hands full serving all our patrons! And I didn't want to put off travel until "someday" and later find out that it never came.

Before the publication of **Double Luck** I'd fled one country, started a new life in Taiwan and then the United States and for family reasons had returned to China once and Taiwan a number of times. I'd also visited Mexico, Spain, Russia and Germany as well as various places in the United States. But my persistent drive to succeed in business had limited the travels that I could undertake.

My rushed trip to see Big Sister had made me acutely conscious of how my life might have turned out had I not left China in 1951. That trip deepened my gratitude for the opportunities I had, and made me determined to seize all the possibilities that I could. My life now was the opposite of the poverty and restrictions of my youth. My good fortune meant I could jump out of the box of the familiar more often and experience other areas and cultures. An old Chinese proverb expresses my belief perfectly: "Traveling thousands of miles is better than reading thousands of books."

I got a similar point of view from Father Ed at St. Timothy's Catholic Church in Morro Bay. He's an educated man who speaks directly and often accompanies tours to the kinds of places I don't have the know-how to visit on my own. I met him when he was new to the area, close to when *Double Luck* came out. Many of my customers were Catholic and they introduced us. We hit it off immediately. I learned that he had known that the priesthood was the right path for him, in the same way that I just knew that The Coffee Pot was right for me. And he views his parishioners as family, in the same way that for me many of my customers are my family. Father Ed regularly welcomes me to church functions and he's introduced me to things like pumpkin and gingerbread lattes. And, I've often traveled with his tour groups.

One of my biggest adventures with him started in Cape Town, South Africa, and ended 1,500 miles north at Victoria Falls. In between was the most exciting part, and the reason many Americans visit Africa. The safari! Nine of us rode in an oversized jeep. As it bumped down rutted tracks, we saw lions, okapi, impala and groups of elephants—fifty at a time! The first elephant we encountered was only seven feet away from us and seemed to be posing for photographs. The guide let us stay that close for a few pictures, then put some space between us and the magnificent but unpredictable animal.

During our days on safari I particularly enjoyed long talks with our tour guide, a vivacious man in his late thirties who had followed his father into the trade. "We are saving to buy two Jeeps," he explained. "Then we will start our own business." He smiled when he said that and so did I, for his determination and willingness to work hard reminded me of my own quest for success. I could absolutely relate to his focus and goal.

Closing the restaurant over the Christmas holidays for three weeks provided a window of time I made good use of. One such trip was a Rhine river cruise to Germany with a group of high school teachers. We visited Christmas markets in several cities. Snow and cobblestoned streets created a gorgeous winter wonderland that I really enjoyed. The locals were so friendly too. At one place I drank a dark, smoky-flavored beer and ate a sausage twice the length of the bun it came in. Thanks to the delicious spiced wine served so often, my memories are a little confused about some of the stops.

Many of my trips involved cruises, to Alaska and Mexico, through the Panama Canal to Spain and several other places. I loved these trips and they made me think that as I aged cruising could be a viable alternative to some kind of retirement home.

I'd seen friends over the years end up in places they hated, surrounded by people on breathing machines, in wheel chairs or behind walkers. That's not the way I want to go. I have no desire to depend on others or to live in what one of my friends called a "warehouse for the elderly waiting to die."

Image 10 Setting off to see color change in New England, with Betty and Bob Beach, ca. 2014

Image 11 Dutch night on a cruise

Cruising is the opposite of that kind of lifestyle. The ships are like small cities, with shops, restaurants, theaters, libraries, spas, pools, game rooms, gyms, and even sports facilities. Luxury surrounds you, people wait on you with big smiles and there's a private verandah on which to sit and relax. Friendly folks clean your room regularly. The food is abundant and if you get tired of one kind of restaurant, there are others to choose from. Room service is available throughout the day and night and you can dress up often. There's good entertainment and there are always people from many different countries to meet and talk with about life, children and grandchildren. There's always something to learn and you can visit different locales without hauling luggage from one hotel to another.

All that sounds ideal to me. So, what I'd love to do if I could afford it is to book cruises as often as possible, for as long as I can. In any case, that's my idea of a path forward. On cruises, in my experience, you grow young.

My philosophy is that you can't think about money when you travel. It will ruin your trip. But I do love a bargain. That's taken me many times to Las Vegas, where the casinos offer luxurious accommodations and lavish buffets at rock-bottom prices to entice people to come and gamble.

Although many Chinese are notorious gamblers, fortunately I am not. I usually play with $40 or $50. When it's gone I enjoy the luxurious surroundings and the entertainment, from Bette Midler on my first visit there to Cirque de Soleil's Zumanity on my most recent one. That show involved all of Cirque's usual astounding acrobatics and music, but very few of their renowned costumes. The performers were mostly nude! Well, as they say, what happens in Vegas stays in Vegas. But it's not a show I'll soon forget! Needless to say, Father Ed was not along on this trip.

Wherever I travelled, I checked out the coffee. In Germany it tended to be stronger than American blends, while in Asia it was quite weak, almost watery. That changed after Starbucks opened stores there in 2000 and after.

A favorite destination of mine, one I've visited three times with Father Ed and one or more of his parishioners, is Thailand. It's a study in contrasts. The luxury hotels and shopping in Bangkok are easy for an American to afford and the food is delicious. But there's another side of life in Thailand. On a river trip in a small narrow boat my fellow travelers and I passed tiny tumbledown wooden houses and witnessed lots of poverty.

As is often the case, seeing such scenes triggered memories of my childhood. "That's how I used to live," I told my travel mate, Joanne Jones. Feeling grateful for my good fortune, I made it a point to tip my chamber "boy" at the hotel every day. He was so lucky, I thought each time I did this, to have a job in the city with food and a roof over his head.

On another occasion we took a side trip into Cambodia to see the ancient historical sites of Angkor Wat and Angkor Thom. Although they are both World Heritage Sites, when Father Ed, Joanne and I were there we were sorry to see that they seemed unprotected. Hordes of tourists tromped the grounds and the surrounding jungle appeared to be creeping back in.

Oddly, though these were ancient Buddhist temples, I didn't get a deeply religious feeling visiting them. My Buddhism, it occurred to me, is now a day-in, day-out practice of goodness and right action rather than formal participation in an organized religion. My behaviors mirror an inner spirit. The fruits of this ingrained way of life, I understood, had already provided much. I did not know it at the time, but so much more was in store for me.

Image 12, 13 In Xinjiang Province, near Mongolia in northwest China, 2018

17
MY DREAM HOUSE

All the attention that **Double Luck** received opened another opportunity besides travel. When a fellow who donated thirty of my books to his daughter's school in Cayucos offered me a house he'd redone at a price I couldn't resist, I sold my Los Osos home for a handsome profit and moved. My new place was just a ten-minute walk from The Coffee Pot. Then the same man suggested that we purchase a large lot on the bluff above the Morro Bay waterfront. We'd split the property and each build ocean-view homes. I loved the idea. I'd be even closer to my restaurant and I could construct a house that reflected my personality and the good fortune I'd created.

Things didn't go well at first. The city denied the application to divide the lot when my business partner applied, so I decided to take the papers in myself. My experience was quite different.

"I've read about you," the friendly clerk said. "You're a generous man with a big heart and I admire you. Let me review the application and I'm sure it will be approved."

And it was. Surely, I thought, this was a sign of more good to come. With a building permit approved, an architect drew up plans that matched my grandiose dreams. I'd once seen a house designed by a Frank Lloyd Wright student and been impressed by the architecture of residences in various cities. I'd also stayed at the beautiful Paris and Bellagio casinos in Las Vegas, and their style influenced my notions too. Once completed in 2005, my dream home pretty much took up the entire lot, was the opposite of everything I'd ever had before and expressed how I viewed my success at the time.

Image 14 Entry Courtyard

The outside resembled an Italian villa while the inside had Asian touches in accordance with Feng Shui principles.

Image 15 Morro Rock from Master Suite

It had two suites. The one on the ground level had a heated floor, a spa and a large shower. The master suite took up the entire second story. It had bamboo flooring, a far cry from the dirt floors of my childhood, a massive shower and a large spa. Both suites had high ceilings, nine-foot-high doors and dramatic ocean and harbor views. Two of the three decks faced the immense and ancient Morro Rock.

Image 16 Kitchen and Living Room

I planned to fill the house with friends and my Coffee Pot "family." And when it was ready, I hosted parties every week. Literally! The number of guests ranged from seven to forty-seven. I supplied red and white wine and created wonderful spreads with roast chicken, veggie and green salads, breadsticks, fruit, and big desserts from Costco. Often there was so much that people left with bags of food.

I loved to bring my friends together and see them mingle in my beautiful new home. Luxurious, clean and spacious, it stood in sharp contrast to how I grew up. I had abundant food to share, friendship, laughter and love. Every night I watched the sun set to the West. My heart overflowed.

Image 17 View from the upper deck of Morro Bay harbor

My good fortune is grand, I often thought to myself. The Coffee Pot is successful. I have the time and money to travel, and I am more and more accustomed to speaking in public.

But then one day in 2007, I think it was, something happened that shook me. I'd given a talk in nearby Arroyo Grande and was heading home on the freeway, traveling along at sixty-five miles per hour. Suddenly I could barely see. I heard cars nearby. My heart thumped. I gripped the wheel, so hard my fingers hurt. I should pull over, I thought. Get off the highway. But I couldn't see the shoulder. A huge truck passed. The noise scared me. Then I saw its shape when it pulled in front of me. I followed it. Blinking, hoping to see more. Fortunately, the truck exited shortly after that, and so did I.

To my relief there was a gas station right there. I pulled in, slammed on the brakes and grabbed my cell phone. But I couldn't see the numbers. I knew something was wrong, but didn't know what. Shaking, I asked one of the station attendants to phone my son and daughter-in-law. They arrived and took me home. Gradually, my sight returned.

A bit later my friend Milt Carrigan called to ask how the talk had gone. When I told him what had happened, he gasped. "Gordon," he said, "that is serious. Get to the emergency room right now. I'll call ahead and tell them you're coming in. Go."

It's a good thing I listened to him. For it turned out that I'd suffered a TIA, a Transient Ischemic Attack. By a magical coincidence, my former doctor saw me. "It's like a mini-stroke," he explained. "A clot in an artery on your neck temporarily cut off the flow of blood to a portion of the brain. In your case it affected the optical nerves." He paused and pursed his lips. "You must take better care of yourself Chi Fa. A TIA often comes before a major stroke."

The next day my own doctor reinforced the message. "What you experienced is a warning sign, one not to be taken lightly." He prescribed several medications and later ordered a stint inserted in the neck artery that had been a problem.

As in so many of my life situations, friends have played a crucial role, stepping in to point me in the right direction. I'm grateful for Milt's quick thinking.

Life, I've learned, is itself a gamble. The TIA, I had to admit, was a wake-up call. I vowed I would take better care of myself. Soon after that I began taking daily walks.

I also thought that perhaps the warning wasn't just about my health. I'd had inklings from time to time that my grand dream of displaying my success might have gone overboard. The monthly payment on the interest-only mortgage was nearly $5000. Still, I believed that if I ever had to sell the house I'd make money. That had been the case with every other residence I'd owned. I knew too that something better would evolve if for some reason my economic situation eventually worsened.

It just turned out that "eventually" came a lot sooner than expected. And with results quite different from what I'd assumed. My "dream" lasted for four wonderful years before it abruptly ended.

18
LEARNING TO TIGHTEN MY BELT

I find that life in America is like this: first you're up, and then you're down. Chinese tradition teaches us to react to both things the same way—wait and see. There is a famous Chinese parable which expresses this truth. An old farmer worked the earth with the help of his son and their plow horse. One day the horse got loose and ran off into the nearby mountains. The man's neighbors said "What bad luck!"

The farmer said "Maybe yes, maybe no. I'll wait and see."

One day when his son was trying to ride a wild horse he fell off and broke his leg. "Oh no," the neighbors said, "Your son won't be able to help you plow. What bad luck!"

The farmer replied "Maybe yes, maybe no. Wait and see."

The next day the army came through the village to conscript young men into military service to fight in the war. They didn't take the farmer's son because of his broken leg. "What good luck!" the farmer's neighbors cried as they watched their own sons led away.

"Maybe yes, maybe no," the farmer said. "Wait and see."

And that parable fits this portion of my story perfectly. I'd built a home that encompassed my dream of grandeur, yet I'd had unrealistic expectations. For when the economy crashed in 2008, that set off a chain of events that changed the direction of my life. The value of my home plummeted. I now owed far more than the house was worth.

In September of 2010 the bank called in my loan. If I couldn't pay it off immediately, they would repossess my house by the end of the month. Many banks at the time rewrote mortgages to give homeowners a break. My bank wouldn't do that, even though my payments were current and I was the original owner. Nor would they give me time to refinance through another lender. Instead, they seized my dream house and sold it.

The bank offered no explanation, an attitude I thought unfair. At the same time, I had to admit that those high monthly payments, plus property taxes and significant upkeep, had been a huge burden and responsibility.

The day I left my dream house for the last time, I had zero feelings. I remembered Big Sister's advice that hard times would pass, and would make me stronger. I told myself that the place had been mine to build and enjoy, but not mine to keep. I told myself I would never look back again. I told myself to move on, to remain detached from the dream. I told myself I had been through worse things before and that I would be a success nonetheless. I told myself that good fortune would be mine again. Wait and see, I told myself.

To simplify my life I hired someone to sell most of my furniture, including some valuable antiques. I had to let go of many things I treasured, including a two hundred year old bamboo bird cage and a piece of jade Good Aunt had given me. This was difficult to do, so having someone else handle the sale was wise. Yet the experience was not a good one; many of my things sold far below market value.

What I learned is that it's important to know the value of your goods and to rely on people with a strong background and reputation.

This was a difficult time for me. I rented a condo near the Catholic Church where my dear friend Father Ed was the priest. Support was just a few steps away, and I sorely needed it for a while.

A few months later, in early 2011, my daughter-in- law Sophie became my partner in The Coffee Pot. I'd been planning to retire but work part of the time and travel as well. She was the business manager for The China Dragon and had been the banquet manager at a classy Chinese restaurant in San Jose, so she had plenty of skills. This allowed me to keep my options open.

The crash affected all aspects of the U.S. economy and caused a slow-down that lasted five years, so my home wasn't the only thing affected. Fewer tourists came to Morro Bay and a number of local people and businesses filed for bankruptcy. Business at The Coffee Pot dropped off as well and that caused me problems too. I feared I'd be unable to pay bills and lose all the good fortune I'd worked so hard to create.

I had worried for some time that I too would have to file for bankruptcy. I pride myself on doing things right, and initially my sense was that I had failed. Cruel words that shaped so much of my childhood resurfaced—"bad boy" "stupid" "worthless" "no good." Anxious and worried, I had difficulty sleeping. Wait and see, I eventually reminded myself. That helped.

And then a friend told me something that made a real difference. He knew I was worried, troubled about something. I finally explained the situation, which wasn't easy for me to do.

He put a hand on my shoulder and smiled. "Gordon," he said, "the goal of bankruptcy "is to give deserving people like you a fresh start. It's not about punishing you for having financial problems, and then holding that against you. It's cleaning the slate and letting you get back to doing what you do well."

After he explained the goal and the process, my shame ebbed away. That's all I need, I thought. Just give me a fresh start and I can put my financial life back in balance. I realized, too, that I was not alone. Many of my fellow citizens, a term I am proud to use, had to do this also.

With the help of my daughter-in-law Sophie and Milt Carrigan, who had been handling correspondence and other tasks for several years, I worked with a bankruptcy lawyer and devised a plan to protect my assets. I purchased a modest home.

Under California law the restaurant, now owned with Sophie, and my residence would be exempt from seizure once I actually filed for bankruptcy.

My new home, in a well-established and quiet manufactured home park on the south edge of town, was half the size of my dream property. The front deck overlooked the mountains, green in winter and brown in summer, not the sea. But I was content. I purchased the home outright. This, finally, was a home that no one ever could take away from me.

We filed for bankruptcy in October 2012 and the process took several months. In the end the trustee ordered the discharge of my debts. I now had a new financial lease on life. A deep sigh of relief swept through my whole body. Once again, I thought, my good fortune.

These events didn't devastate me; they were a wakeup call, similar in a sense to what happened when China Diner failed. It caused me to examine my actions and admit that my dreams of what success meant had caused me to act unwisely. I had known from the start that my dream house was a risk. I'd had four great years living there and now it was time to redefine what success meant. I set my grief aside and began enjoying a simpler life. There was no stress, no financial pressure, no outrageous overhead costs. I was older and wiser, and I still had my beloved Coffee Pot.

I decided I would do just one thing well. I would not expand by adding more restaurants as I had done in Manhattan Beach. I would not live in a grand house where I had to come up with a huge mortgage payment. In short, I would not try to get bigger and bolder, thinking that this would make me more successful. It was time to scale back my American dream and enjoy the slower pace of my Chinese heritage.

I would continue to travel when I could afford it, enjoy meals out at Kevin and Sophie's restaurant, and meet my friends at a weekly dining club rather than having them over to my dream house for a lavish spread. No one seemed to mind. We were happy enjoying each other's company.

19
CREATING COMMUNITY

I have owned and run The Coffee Pot for nearly three decades now, and it has made me very happy. When I wake in the morning I look forward to each day, knowing that I will see friends and perhaps meet new ones.

My little restaurant is just off the waterfront next to a souvenir and tee shirt shop and in front of Giovanni's Fish Market. From the start I've tried to make it a friendly spot where every guest is welcome and senses the good energy here. I greet customers personally. Those I know well get a big hug too. If anyone has to wait for a table, I take them fresh coffee as they sit on a bench outside. I know that waiting for breakfast or lunch isn't always easy, so I do my best to make it a bit easier.

Kindness and good service, I believe, win tremendous customer response. When people get these they often return, and many of those who do have become friends. Such customers looked for breakfast and found a community as well. This is one of the most precious blessings I've received. There is definitely a family feel to The Coffee Pot. It has become my permanent home, my source of many friendships and much joy. Some of my local customers even help out with needed repairs, making my life much easier.

One of my regulars has been eating at The Coffee Pot two to four times a week for over two decades. A Los Osos couple has been coming daily for over twenty years. The Coffee Pot is now a second home for them, and for many others. Visitors from the Central Valley return every summer, and I consider many to be friends as well as customers. I often sit down and sip some coffee with such folks. I enjoy getting to know them, and I hope the reverse is true.

After a while I started introducing my regulars to each other. All retired, they were pretty much in the same age range although their tastes and interests varied widely. There was a former Wall Street executive and his wife, a professor/professional guitar player, a couple from Las Vegas, an English couple, a retired city building inspector, a Hewlett-Packard engineer, a couple who had lived in Morro Bay for fifty years, and another couple who had been farmers in the Central Valley.

No matter their backgrounds, they all found a lively common ground in The Coffee Pot. For many the restaurant has become a kind of social center, and for the widowers and widows in town it can be a lifeline. We go through the losses of members of our group together. If you are lucky enough to grow old you will understand this. Beloved friends die and you need people you can reach out to for common comfort.

**Image 18 With Patricia Wood, a good friend
and a customer for over fifteen years**

The other day Sid, one of my regulars, said "this place reminds me of Cheers. You know, that bar on the TV show? In Boston?" I must have looked blank. "That show from the Eighties? The place 'Where Everybody Knows Your Name'? This is Morro Bay's Cheers!" The others at his table nodded and grinned. I was baffled. "Except here you can bring your grand kids," added Sid's wife Beryl, "and you order Belgian waffles for them, not beer."

I smiled and went to check on other tables, carrying my coffee pot with me. As my old friends continued to laugh and talk about the similarities between my little restaurant and an imaginary bar three thousand miles away, it occurred to me that the way they know The Coffee Pot is different from the way I know it.

From what I can tell, people see this as a warm and friendly restaurant where they can meet with friends to eat good food. They see me as "a connector of people" who's created "a friendly place" and "makes everyone feel special." People tell me these and many other beautiful things directly or in letters.

I see what they mean, and yet for me The Coffee Pot is a place where I can repay the kindness paid to me during an otherwise miserable childhood and youth. The hardships I experienced taught me to cherish goodness in others and to do all I could to treat others well.

In retrospect, I understand that this is a Buddhist notion I'm acting on: our thoughts and actions shape the kind of life we have. If we do good things, in the future good things will happen to us—and to our children and grandchildren. And the reverse is true too.

Image 19 With Mei Lei, daughter of Jeff & Karen Root

There are times when my grasp of English remains a bit rough, particularly when it comes to idioms. Marge Reinhart, a vivacious and young-at-heart friend for years, recalled an incident that reflects this perfectly. "One morning I went in and Gordon slipped his arm around my waist and walked me over to a table to introduce me to some new customers. I was a little alarmed as I could see the two elderly ladies had a Bible between them. He said, quite cheerfully, 'I'd like you to meet Marge, she's my hot mamma!' Now, I knew Gordon meant that I was his good friend, but the two women froze. They didn't say a word. Long seconds ticked by. Then I steered Gordon away from them, and had to laugh out loud. I explained what 'hot mama' meant in English, and ever since that day he calls me 'hot mama' and he says he's my 'hot papa.' It does my spirits good!"

**Image 20 With Marge Reinhart, a close friend
since I've lived in Morro Bay**

Another customer, Jim from Las Vegas, has captured something of what I aim for. "Gordon makes everyone feel special. His heart is always in the right place. If you didn't

special. His heart is always in the right place. If you didn't know about his terrible childhood, you'd never know he went through such neglect and abuse. It doesn't show on him, and it doesn't show in the way he treats people."

Image 21 With Professor George Griener

Images 22 & 23 Regular customers and their families

Sometimes the things my friends say about me seem unreal. Is this all true? Who paid them to say this? Then I laugh and give thanks for my wonderful friends. I think as well of them as they do of me. We are blessed. This is my good fortune.

20
BUILDING FOR THE NEXT GENERATION

Filial piety, an ancient core value in China, teaches children to respect, obey and care for their parents—and ancestors. My experience and observations suggest that the basic approach to childhood is quite different in America. Here people focus on giving overwhelming love and support to their children and grandchildren. My circumstances as a child provided few positive lessons. During my impoverished youth my parents and grandparents were dead. I had no real role model for how to behave toward my children. I was nearly eight thousand miles away when my sons grew up.

But my life has changed. I have learned how to provide praise and encouragement for my sons and grandchildren in the American tradition. It hasn't always been easy because of distances.

Both of my sons have dual citizenship which has allowed them to travel back and forth without having to worry about visas expiring. That's particularly the case for my older son Jason. After studying English while staying with me in Los Osos, he moved to San Jose and then to Las Vegas. He became a dealer and eventually ended up at a high end casino, as did his wife. In 2002 they used the money they'd saved to invest in mainland China properties. They eventually moved back to Taiwan with their daughter Emilie, and recently returned to San Jose temporarily. Although we keep in touch and they are important to me, unfortunately we do not see each other often.

Kevin and Sophie moved to this area in 2007 after about a decade in San Jose and have lived in nearby Los Osos since then. More about them shortly.

As I watch my sons building their careers, pride fills my heart for they have created their own good fortunes. And as I think about my grandchildren, I give thanks often that none of them have experienced the hardships I endured as a child. And I am overjoyed that all of them are educated. Kevin's son Eddie spoke only Chinese until he went to kindergarten. A gifted student, he now translates for Sophie's parents, reads beyond his grade level and spends six hours a week with math and English tutors. Kevin's other son, Aaron, is now seventeen and in high school in Taiwan. Jason's daughter Emilie, a beautiful young lady, is also in high school. She's bilingual and has attended both Buddhist and Catholic schools.

Image 21 Grandchildren Emilie, Eddie and Aaron, in about 2014

In March 2017, the building that houses Kevin and Sophie's China Dragon in North Morro Bay sold. The new owner jacked up the rent and demanded that they agree to it or move out. They knew they couldn't make enough extra money to pay what he required. Bad luck? As the old Chinese farmer would have said, "Maybe yes, maybe no. Wait and see."

Fortuitously, the owners of the only other Chinese restaurant in Morro Bay decided to retire and wanted Kevin and Sophie to take over their place. This was an amazing opportunity and a huge challenge. The new restaurant was larger. It seated ninety-five compared to thirty-six, and included a banquet room as well as a patio with room for twenty-five more people. The old China Dragon was in the residential part of town. It had lots of regular customers, but little walk-in traffic. This new place had regular clientele too, but chiefly for its all-you-can-eat buffet. Its prime location on Morro Bay's scenic and charming Embarcadero meant lots of walk-ins. It also had its own parking lot, a real bonus for a business in that area.

Sophie and I discussed the opportunity and the hazards. She knew I had been down this road before, having to decide whether to expand, make big menu changes and take on all the risks involved. Her hope for the new place was to give their patrons an experience of China. She wanted to remove the stereotypical Chinese buffet, improve the ambience and turn it into a sit-down restaurant that offered quality foods, including popular options like Boba tea, dim sum and plenty of vegetarian dishes.

Of course, with big hopes come big fears. I could understand that. I also knew that Kevin and Sophie were smart and energetic, and that the opportunity and location were golden. Hundreds of people visit Morro Bay every day and most stroll the Embarcadero with its art galleries, shops, restaurants, cafes, tour boat operators, barking sea lions and fabulous harbor views.

I advised Sophie and Kevin to go for it, knowing that they would time improvements with care. They took the plunge and signed the lease. We talked about everything from décor to kitchen equipment and the new menu. Sophie and I visited Chinese restaurants and supermarkets in San Jose and Los Angeles and checked out restaurant supply stores to learn about new equipment and supplies.

I dearly want the new China Dragon to be Kevin and Sophie's good fortune. I hope it also will become a social center in the same way that The Coffee Pot has. They're still young and if they continue to work as they have, their future will be bright.

What I have learned is that people come to a restaurant for the welcome, not just the food. Perhaps that's true with every successful venture in life. The heart you put into something is just as important as the expertise with which you do it.

21
LIFE, LIBERTY AND THE PURSUIT OF HAPPINESS

You can walk away from bad experiences, but they don't walk away from you. Some are too deeply rooted. When I was very little, people feared that the Japanese would come and take all the children and pregnant women from their homes and shoot them. I used to hide inside layers and layers of prickly straw crawling with bugs. When I first stayed at Big Sister's I hid in a storage room whenever her husband was home. It was dark, lacked fresh air, and mosquitoes bit me. But I had to stay still, silent as a corpse. My crime? I was a boy, but not *brother-in-law's* boy.

Even today darkness is not my friend. Sometimes I have nightmares. I sleep with the TV on for light and the low hum of human companionship. My conscious mind can understand why Big Sister had to lock me up in the dark. It can understand why my sister-in-law sold me and why Big Brother beat me, even stole my money. But my unconscious mind rules the nights and occasionally I am once again three, four or five, claustrophobic and terrified.

Telling my story to others, in my memoir **Double Luck** and at schools and colleges, has been therapeutic. It is an emotional experience every time I talk, and it helps. Creating an extended family through The Coffee Pot has been healing too. People arrive for a meal and greet me with hugs. As a child, I yearned for that kind of affection. Now I have it.

America is everything I ever hoped for. It is my good fortune. Still, part of the hurt done to me as a child will probably affect me forever. If so, I can handle that. Two sayings of the Buddha guide me. The first is that "Happiness will never come to those who fail to appreciate what they already have." The second, which Big Sister and Good Auntie told me in different ways, is that "Remembering a wrong is like carrying a burden on the mind." I do my best to be thankful for all that I have and to leave behind the wrongs done to me in the past.

I still travel to schools and colleges to talk about my nightmare childhood in China and to offer American kids a glimpse of an altogether different kind of life. They seem to take in my story and think about it. They see that I survived hardship and have done well. I hope this inspires them to work hard, to persevere and to live their dreams. I hope they learn, too, that poverty and even abuse aren't excuses for not succeeding. You will overcome the trials of a hard childhood, I tell them, and challenges will remain. Life won't always go your way. You'll have to find the strength and the right attitude to adjust to it. If you work hard and respect yourself and others, I tell "my" students, there is nothing but good opportunity.

Image 24 Celebrating the 2018 Christmas Season at nearby Hearst Castle with close friends

In China I desperately longed for a safe, secure place to live. In America I have that. In China my family and I—and many, many people around me—starved. In America I am a restaurant owner and feed hundreds of people each week. Once I was deeply ashamed because I had so little formal education. Now I go into schools and colleges to share the story of my life and the lessons I have learned. People treat me with respect, admiration and affection. You simply never know where life can take you.

For all the material good fortune I have had, what has come to mean more to me has been sharing my story in hopes that others could learn from it. Doing this has become a passion, one that has taken me many places in California. What I did not know was that people observed this activity and wanted to honor me for it.

In January 2019 the Morro Bay Chamber of Commerce named me a "Living Treasure." My good friend Father Ed Holterhoff introduced me at the award dinner. "I have joked with Gordon for years," he said, "that I have to walk behind him for all the good he has done. He is a remarkable man."

I had difficulty staying calm as Father Ed continued to praise me as "an example for this community and America today." His words, and this honor, left me deeply touched. All my sacrifices and hard work flashed through my mind, and I hoped others would understand that they too could realize their dreams.

As if this were not enough, I learned that in March of 2019 I would be the featured author at the Huntington Beach Reads One Book event. A library committee chooses a single book for the entire community to read, and ***Double Luck*** is the one for this year. Coming on top of the Morro Bay award, this recognition left me quite stunned and happy.

As a child I could imagine that silver dragons would carry me through the sky, far from pain and poverty, but I could never have dreamed all the blessings that would one day be mine here in America. Big Sister told me that good fortune would find me. And it has.

AFTERWORD

In addition to the wonderful awards I've received recently, my greatest blessings have been the reactions to *Double Luck*. Questions from students and letters and cards from many people have touched me deeply. People refer to my "courage and persistence." They can't fathom how I experienced so many "heartaches and tribulations" yet remain trusting and kind. They refer to my "courage," my "intuitiveness" and my "strong and enduring spirit." They mention my "eternal optimism and faith in mankind." And they call *Double Luck* a "testimony of survival and persistence."

Such statements humble me, but I am overjoyed when people tell me how my experience has affected them and altered their way of thinking. A young mother, for instance, said that my story taught her "to embrace the simple and pure things in life . . . ." Others say that they learned the importance of not holding grudges and about the power of forgiveness and kindness. A young student wrote that "you need to let things go and not hold them inside because that will only hurt you."

Most often people mention that they learned from my story to "be grateful" and appreciate what they have. Sometimes this was quite personal. A young woman wrote that even though her parents are divorced, she can be grateful that she does have parents who love her. Most often people expressed appreciation for being in the United States. Reading about my childhood, they say, made them aware that they cannot take for granted the freedoms they enjoy here.

One of my favorite questions came from a student who asked if I thought hardships can be bad and good at the same time. "Yes," I said. By the time I was seven I had to rely on myself, a situation that forced me to grow up quickly and appreciate life a lot more. As Big Sister told me, "difficulty will educate you." So, I do think that hardships can be both good and bad. It depends on how you think about them and what you do with them.

And that is the key. Attitude is the crucial ingredient. Poverty and hardships do not need to crush you. Neither do small problems. Every day at The Coffee Pot I see examples of that. Someone my age comes in, sits down and orders a cup of coffee. In the bowl on the table there are regular sugar, and pink and yellow packets of sugar substitutes. The person says "What, no raw sugar! I'm out of here."

This happens with all kinds of things. Maybe they think the butter doesn't taste right, or that the bacon is too well done. So they leave, and they don't get to see what a warm and friendly place The Coffee Pot is. I say to myself, people in my generation are old enough to know how precious life is. But too often they don't fully understand this. They make little things into big things. You can't tell them to appreciate the heart that goes into the restaurant, the effort to make the service special. They have left already, and their attitude has created their own hardship.

TIME LINE

1942 December 13, Lu Chi Fa born, Jiangsu Province China	Japan occupies much of China through WWII; a long-running civil war simmers.
1944 Both parents die	
1945	WWII ends, civil war hostilities resume.
1949	Chinese Communists win, form People's Republic of China; Chiang Kai-shek flees to Taiwan
1950	June, Korean War starts; October, China enters Korean War
1951 Flees to Hong Kong	
1952 Lives in refugee camps, begs on street	November, Dwight Eisenhower elected President
1953 Makes it to Taiwan	July, Korean War ends
1957 Works at American officers' club	
1960	November, John F. Kennedy elected President
1961-63 Military service in Taiwan	
1963 Starts work at NCO club, Taichung	November, Kennedy assassinated
1964	November, Lyndon Johnson elected president
1965 Marries Vivian	U.S. Immigration and Naturalization Act
1966 December, son Jason born	Cultural Revolution starts in China
1968 September, son Kevin born	Tet Offensive in Vietnam; November, Richard Nixon elected President
1969 October, emigrates to California	March, Sino-Soviet Border Conflict; July, Apollo 11 lands on moon
1970 Gets student visa	

1971 Works in Denver, gets green card; returns to Taiwan for family	UN recognizes People's Republic of China; Republic of China (Taiwan) expelled
1972 December, age 30	February, President Nixon visits China; November, Nixon reelected
1973	May, Senate Watergate Committee begins hearings
1974 To Taiwan hoping family will join him in U.S.	August, Nixon resigns as President; Gerald Ford becomes President
1975	April, Chiang Kai-shek dies; Vietnam War ends
1976	Cultural Revolution ends in China; November, Jimmy Carter elected President
1977 Purchases first U.S. home, Santa Ana	
1978 Opens China Diner	
1979	President Carter gives full diplomatic recognition to China, drops official recognition of Republic of China (Taiwan), but promises protection. November, Iran hostage crisis
1980 China Diner fails	March, U.S. boycotts Summer Olympics to protest Soviet invasion of Afghanistan
1980-82 Bartending in Orange County	1982 July, Reagan assures Taiwan
1983 Becomes U.S. citizen	
1984 Buys Manhattan Beach house; China Express opens.	Summer Olympics in Los Angeles; President Reagan reelected
1986 Visits Big Sister in China	January, Space Shuttle Challenger explodes
1987 Buys USA Croissant	June, President Reagan in Berlin challenges Soviet Union to "tear down this wall"
1988 Buys third food court place	November, George H.W. Bush elected President
1989	June Tiananmen Square Massacre; November, Berlin Wall comes down

1990 Sells all three businesses in Los Angeles County, travels to Russia and Germany. Visits Morro Bay and buys The Coffee Pot.	The Soviet Union is in turmoil. May, Boris Yeltsin elected president of Russian Federation; August, Iraq invades Kuwait
1992 Sells Manhattan Beach house; buys Los Osos house	November, Bill Clinton elected President
1993 Jason arrives	
1994 Kevin arrives	January, Northridge earthquake in Los Angeles
1996	March, first free Presidential vote Taiwan
1999 Karen Grencik proposes memoir, introduces Becky White	April, Columbine High School massacre
2000	October, President Clinton signs trade relations agreement with China; November, George W. Bush is elected President
2001 *Double Luck* published; meets Father Ed; starts talks to local groups	September 11, terrorists hijack four airplanes; Afghanistan invaded
2002 *Double Luck* receives gold award from Parents' Choice Foundation	
2003	March, U.S. invasion of Iraq
2004 Business partner Bob leaves	February, Facebook launched; November, George W. Bush reelected
2005 Builds dream house. Starts talks at Taft College	August, Hurricane Katrina
2007 Starts talks at Cal Poly University	December, Great Recession starts.
2008	China becomes largest U.S. foreign creditor; November, Barack Obama elected President
2009	Great Recession deepens
2010 Loses dream home	China becomes second largest economy in the world
2011 Sophie becomes a partner in The Coffee Pot; buys small home	

2012 October, files for bankruptcy; December, Chi Fa turns 70	November, Obama reelected
2016	November, Donald Trump elected President
2017 March, Kevin and Sophie buy Embarcadero restaurant in Morro Bay	
2019 January, Honored as a Living Treasure of Morro Bay. March, Lu Chi Fa is featured author at Huntington Beach Reads One Book event	

OTHER PHOTOS

Image 25 Lu Chi Fa in 1999 Image 26 Lu Chi Fa 1977, 1988 and 2009

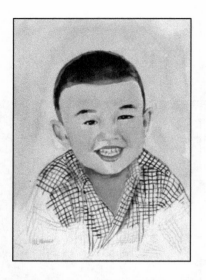

Image 27 Grandson Eddie, age about four

Image 28 Grandson Eddie, age 9

HONORS

When the Morro Bay Chamber of Commerce named me a Living Treasure, this represented a highpoint in my life. It touched me deeply.

A PROCLAMATION OF THE CITY COUNCIL
OF THE CITY OF MORRO BAY RECOGNIZING
THE MORRO BAY CHAMBER OF COMMERCE
2018 "LIVING TREASURE"

WHEREAS, the Morro Bay Living Treasure is selected for a body of work and service provided to Morro Bay by lifestyle over a lifetime; and

WHEREAS, Lu Chi Fa -- known to Morro Bay residents as Gordon Lu -- has owned and operated the Coffee Pot Restaurant on Front Street for 25 years; and

WHEREAS, Mr. Lu is known for his affable disposition and personal service given to local Morro Bay residents and visitors alike; and

WHEREAS, Mr. Lu is more than a businessman alone—he shared his inspiring life story in a co-authored biography called "Double Luck" that is read by students in every city and school in the State of California; and

WHEREAS, the revenue generated by book sales has raised tens of thousands of dollars which he donates to local libraries; and

WHEREAS, in the words of Father Edward Holterhoff of St. Timothy's Catholic Church, himself a past recipient of the Citizen of the Year award, "Gordon is a quiet, unassuming, generous man" who is "a role model for our times – a genuine living treasure."

NOW THEREFORE, BE IT RESOLVED that the City of Morro Bay does hereby recognize and proclaim that Gordon Lu has been selected as the Morro Bay Chamber of Commerce 2018 Living Treasure.

IN WITNESS WHEREOF I have hereunto set my hand and caused the seal of the City of Morro Bay to be affixed this 11th day of January 2019

JOHN HEADDING, Mayor
City of Morro Bay, California

STATE OF CALIFORNIA

CERTIFICATE OF RECOGNITION

Presented to:

Lu Chi Fa (Gordon Lu)

In honor of receiving the:

2018 Living Treasure Award
Morro Bay Chamber of Commerce

Dated this 11th day of January, 2019;

WILLIAM W. MONNING
17TH SENATE DISTRICT
CALIFORNIA STATE LEGISLATURE

CERTIFICATE OF RECOGNITION

Gordon Lu

In Honor Of

your excellence and dedication to the
Central Coast community
Morro Bay Chamber of Commerce
2018 Living Treasure

January 11, 2019

Assemblyman Jordan Cunningham
35th District

Certificate of Special Congressional Recognition

Presented to
Lu Chi Fa
Living Treasure

in recognition of outstanding and invaluable
service to the community.

January 11, 2019
DATE

MEMBER OF CONGRESS

DONATIONS OF MY MEMOIR TO CHINESE LIBRARIES

Over the years, I have donated copies of ***Double Luck*** to various libraries in China. That says a lot about how much has changed there since I visited Big Sister in 1986.

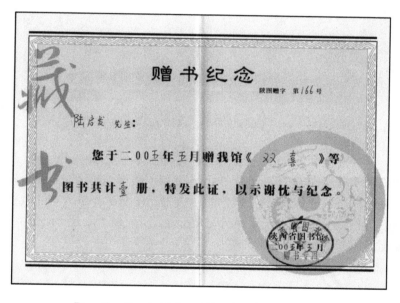

Donation Receipt 1 Sanxi Province library, 2005

荣誉证书

陆启发　先生：

　　承蒙惠赠《双喜》珍贵图书1册。您的捐赠丰富了高邮市图书馆的馆藏，为读者提供了新的知识信息。谨致敬意，并赠本证书惠存。

高邮市图书馆

二〇一三年六月

Donation Receipt 2 Gaoyao library, Gansu province, China 2013

There's a story here. A Chinese couple visiting The Coffee Pot several years ago turned out to be from a town near where I'd been born in 1942. I gave them two copies of Double Luck and asked them if they'd donate one to the library in my hometown. And they did.

收藏证书

兹收到陆启发先生捐赠的图书《Double Luck 双喜》1 册。该书丰富了我馆馆藏，为读者提供了宝贵的知识信息。特发此证，以资谢谌！

青岛市图书馆
2015 年 12 月 15 日

Donation Receipt 3 Library in Shandong Province, Quindao city, 2015

Donation Receipt 4 Xiamen University, China, June 2018

Donation Receipt 5 Guangdong University of Foreign Studies, Guangzhou, China, 2018

IMAGE CREDITS

Cover	Dragon by konsky, via Shutterstock
Image 1	Lu Chi Fa collection
Image 2	Lu Chi Fa collection
Image 3	Lu Chi Fa collection
Image 4	Photo for green card
Image 5	Lu Chi Fa Collection
Image 6	Lu Chi Fa Collection
Image 7	For Naturalization Certificate
Image 8	Courtesy Azul Hull
Image 9	Photo by David Middlecamp/The Tribune "Courtesy of the San Luis Obispo County Tribune"
Image 9	Lu Chi Fa collection
Image 10	Courtesy Bob and Betty Beach
Image 11	Lu Chi Fa collection
Image 12	Lu Chi Fa collection
Photo 13	Lu Chi Fa collection
Photo 14	Photo by Lorin Lee Cary
Photo 15	Photo by Lorin Lee Cary

Photo 16	Photo by Lorin Lee Cary
Photo 17	Photo by Lorin Lee Cary
Photo 18	Courtesy of Pat wood
Photo 19	Courtesy Jeff and Karen Root
Photo 20	Courtesy of Marjorie Reinhardt
Photo 21	Courtesy of Professor George Griener
Photo 22	Lu Chi Fa collection
Photo 23	Lu Chi Fa collection
Photo 24	Photo by PhotogenicInk, Lu Chi Fa collection
Photo 25	Portrait by Al Musso
Photo 26	Portrait by Al Musso
Photo 27	Portrait by Al Musso
Photo 28	Lu Chi Fa collection
Photo 29	Photo by Sandprints Photography, Morro Bay, California

ABOUT THE AUTHORS

Born in China in 1942 and orphaned as a child, Lu Chi Fa fled to Hong Kong and then Taiwan for a better life. In 1969 he immigrated to the U.S., worked in Southern California and ran several successful businesses there. In 1990 he moved to Morro Bay, California where he has owned The Coffee Pot restaurant for nearly thirty years.

His 2001 book, with Becky White, *Double Luck: Memoirs of a Chinese Orphan,* won a gold award from Parents' Choice Foundation. He has told his story at schools and colleges throughout California. In 2019 the Morro Bay Chamber of Commerce honored him as a "Living Treasure" and the Huntington Beach Reads One Book event selected him as the featured author.

Dr. Lorin Lee Cary taught history at the University of Toledo, was a Fulbright Senior Scholar at the University of New South Wales and co-authored *No Strength Without Union* and *Slavery in North Carolina;* both won the Ohio Academy of History's annual Publication Award (1984, 1996). He has published two novels, ***The Custer Conspiracy*** (2009) and ***California Dreaming*** (2017) and is a prize-wining photographer.

Photo 29 Lu Chi Fa and Lorin Lee Cary